DATE DUE

GAYLORD			PRINTED IN U.S.A.

COALITION OR CHAOS?

Books by Roger W. Babson

THE NEW DILEMMA
A BUSINESS MAN'S CREED
INSTINCTS AND EMOTIONS
WHAT IS SUCCESS?
NEW TASKS FOR OLD CHURCHES
MAKING GOOD IN BUSINESS
THE FUTURE OF THE CHURCHES
FUNDAMENTALS OF PROSPERITY

COALITION OR CHAOS?

By

ROGER W. BABSON

*President of Babson's Statistical Organization, Incorporated,
and Moderator of the National Council of the
Congregational and Christian Churches*

NEW YORK

Fleming H. Revell Company

LONDON AND EDINBURGH

Printed in the United States of America

New York: 158 Fifth Avenue
London: 21 Paternoster Square

DEDICATED

TO

REVEREND EVERETT R. CLINCHY

DIRECTOR OF THE

NATIONAL CONFERENCE OF JEWS AND CHRISTIANS

INTRODUCTION

DURING the World War of 1914-1918 one of the most famous posters used by the United States was a simple picture of a child sitting on a man's lap. The child looks up into the man's face and says:

"Daddy, what did *you* do in the War?"

Sooner or later the day is surely coming when one of *my* family is going to ask the following question:

"How did daddy"—or perhaps, granddaddy—"do his bit in the war our nation waged against threatening chaos?"

This book is an answer to that question. Before plunging into the subject, however, may I indulge in some frank reminiscences? (Our impending troubles today are deeply concerned with the economic cycle.) My first venture in life, some twenty-five years ago, was an attack on the business cycle. By gathering and publishing statistics on fundamental conditions, I hoped to provide some protection against the crazy booms which cause the deadly depressions. That is largely a protective service.

Forewarned is forearmed. If people can be told when fundamental conditions have become hazardous and a panic impends, then they can take steps to safeguard themselves. Such caution, exercised by persons who are well informed, will help to moderate speculative excesses. By providing a brake for the boom, we provide a dashpot or shock-absorber for the crash. Thus the prudence of the wise helps to save the reckless from the full penalty of their folly. Just as we cannot act *foolishly* without *hurting* everybody, we cannot act *wisely* without *helping* everybody.

I gradually learned that something more is needed than forecasting the movements of the business cycle from recovery to prosperity, from over-extension to decline and depression. Such work is *protective*. Beneath that is the deeper need for work that is *preventive*. This led me to a growing interest in economic education. It resulted in the founding of Babson Institute for Men; and later, with Mrs. Babson, in establishing Webber College for Women. Both of these institutions are thriving, and we hope that no academic success will ever obscure the vision. *This vision was that the nation needs a nucleus, a spreading and leavening body of young men and women grounded in economics and inspired by spiritual ideals.*

For some years I have been studying, to assist in promoting, along sound lines, the growth of "Consumerism." Much of this so-called consumers' movement is still in the laboratory stage. The various groups approaching it from different angles have much to learn. Nevertheless, it has vast possibilities,—this basic idea, that to save consumers is to save all. This study has greatly interested me in the use, during emergencies, of a *coalition* government. I advance this, however, not as a panacea, a cure-all, a single specific, but rather as a temporary means to an end.

America will at times be faced by an issue of life or death. The potential crisis ahead then is too grave for us to depend upon any single sector or salient.

To drive home this viewpoint, I have written this book. Now once more into action: to strike some blows in the great, good cause of Coalition. It is an accelerating crisis. The tension is constantly tightening. Time has become the essence. Coalition or Chaos,—which will overtake us first? Let me add that in this study Mr. Clarence N. Stone has aided.

ROGER W. BABSON.

Babson Park, Florida,
February 1, 1938.

CONTENTS

I

ARE WE TO FOLLOW SPAIN OR ENGLAND?

THOSE who have visited Madrid do not have to be told of its beauties. It is one of the most attractive and glamorous cities in Europe. Its broad streets, magnificent buildings and numerous parks made it a mecca for both tourists and students of history. It had been especially attractive since the World War, from which Spain prospered financially. It is also believed that the radical government which ruled Spain after the fall of Alfonso cleaned up the city and made it more livable than ever before. The city grew to a population of about 600,000 up to the civil war of 1936.

The center of the old city is the Puerta del Sol, named after one of the famous gates. From this plaza ten old streets radiate. One of these, the Calle de Alcalá, was especially popular with tourists. It will be remembered as the street lined by acacia trees. Several prominent buildings border the plaza, on the south side of which is the Palacio de la Gobernacion. Along Calle de Alcalá is the Academia de Bellas Artes, the Bank of Spain, and Buen Retiro Gardens. All who have been to Madrid well remember the House of Commons on the Plaza de las Cortes. The Plaza Mayor was also an attraction for travelers. Here took place everything from bull fights to coronations.

The leading shops were on Calle de Carretas, Carrera de San Jeronimo, and Calle de la Montera. The luxury and beauty of their merchandise have been the envy of the world. Along these and other streets were numerous churches. Among these will be remembered the Basilica de Nuestra Senora de Atocha, founded in 1523, the Church of San Isidro el Real, and the Church of San Jeronimo el Real. Of the noteworthy secular buildings we love to think of the Palacio Real, which was the royal palace; the Real Museo de Pinturas, which held many of the world's famous pictures; and the Biblioteca Nacional, where one could find some of the world's most ancient and valuable books. The University of Madrid will also be remembered.

Madrid was founded by the Arabs in the tenth century, but it was the fifteenth century before it became a center of learning, art and commerce. The old city was surrounded by a wall, portions of which still remain. Within recent years there was a great development outside of the city walls. Here the well-to-do people built beautiful homes on the new broad streets and squares. Before the civil war these villas were surrounded by gay gardens; the boulevards were lined with beautiful trees; new public buildings were built generously. These formed a striking contrast to old Madrid. In another direction, outside of the old city walls, grew up the industrial section of the city. Here were found the great tobacco factories and other industries which have made Madrid famous among connoisseurs of civic achievement. When the civil war broke out Madrid was noteworthy for jewelry, porcelain, leather goods, musical instruments, baskets and everything that adorns a woman or a home, from fans to sunshades.

WHAT THE CIVIL WAR IS DOING

Following 1936 the situation entirely changed. It became difficult to believe that Madrid was once a gay city. To say nothing of jewelry, musical instruments and sunshades, Madrid went into a tailspin where it had no soap, no tobacco, and no milk. During the civil war Madrid has been thrown back to barbarism. Riches, luxury, comfort, and even common decency are wiped out. Poverty, crime, and disease are now rampant everywhere. Certainly this should be a lesson to dictators and to nations which are now building bombing planes and talking about "another European war." Nearly all the buildings mentioned above have been damaged by shells; some thirty-five hundred innocent people have been killed; perhaps twenty thousand have been wounded. Many of these were wounded while standing in breadlines, clutching at their empty baskets.

Those who have visited Spain during the civil war tell me that the great city markets soon became empty, while the public markets were used for training grounds and hospitals. By decree it became illegal to butcher a cow; while the soldiers in the field had a first call upon the milk. Lemons and onions were the only vegetables that one could buy without special permission. Parents, separated from their children in the morning, never knew at nightfall whether their children would be found at home, or found wounded on the pavement, or found dead in the public morgue.

Even the residents of the city seemed to spend their time fighting with one another or marching about in endless processions rather than doing anything constructive. "Because," they said, "whatever we make or raise will be taken away from us." War posters were seen everywhere, even though the newspapers, on account of paper shortage, were reduced to either two or four pages.

Yet the population of Madrid did not change much during the civil war. The inhabitants knew no safer place to go; while the refugees from the provinces arrived by the thousand. There was a tremendous leveling of classes. This, however, was not accomplished by bringing the poor people up to a higher level, but by eliminating the upper classes and by leveling off the middle classes to the lowest degree. This, moreover, applied to the buildings as well as to the people. Whole sections of the city were abandoned or partly destroyed. The windows of the fine shops remained broken; tramps ran through doorways of buildings once guarded by footmen. There was no regulation of traffic, because private automobiles ceased to exist. Mule carts again replaced motor trucks; and most of the goods were carried on the heads and backs of those too old or too weak to go to the front.

During the civil war few business statistics have come from Spain; apparently bartering is the common form of business. Tobacco and soap are used as money. Nevertheless, although the great stores were closed, the old Moorish bazaars and the street peddlers returned. In other words, the improvements which had been developed through civilization were wiped out; while the people reverted to barbarism and the customs of centuries ago.

Of course, the great railroad stations were closed during the early months of the civil war, when the last trains left Madrid. The famous North Station was completely burned out, although I am told that the clock still stands,—the hands pointing to 11:45, indicating the hour when a portion of a shell stopped this clock, on November 7, 1937. Street traffic ceased each night at 10:00 P.M.; no street lights were ever available, and the windows had to be blackened. Although it was always possible to get a letter in and out of Madrid during these months, the mail had to be trucked nearly three hundred miles, always subject to bombing by the enemy. A few second-rate hotels, where meals were served to those having special food cards, remained open. Communistic dining rooms, serving only soup and bread, replaced the grand restaurants with which travelers are acquainted. The best hotels became hospitals and their beautiful ballrooms public sick wards. The odor of anesthetics took the place of perfume, while pain replaced luxury.

WHAT ABOUT ENGLAND?

The history of England reaches back to about the same date as the history of Spain. England, like Spain, was originally Catholic. For many centuries England was far behind Spain in education, art, commerce, and industry. Spanish ships were sailing all over the world when English commerce had just started. Christopher Columbus was backed by a

Spanish queen,—not by an English queen. The Spanish made the first settlements in America and could have remained in control of this great continent. It is most significant to students of history that the national language of the United States today is not Spanish but English. Why should London become a greater city than Madrid? Why did a small group of English people become possessors of the greater portion of the earth? Why did Great Britain displace Spain in its world dominions? The answer to these questions is a fitting introduction to this book.

Probably the most significant difference between Spain and England, or Madrid and London, is the relative religion of the people and the effect of this religion on their character. In this connection I am not discussing or comparing the Catholic and Protestant beliefs. Experience has taught me that there is little, if any, relationship between a man's behavior and his theology. Kindliness and honesty, selfishness and brutality can be found among both the most orthodox and the most liberal. Strange to say, the *beliefs* of the people have little effect upon their character, their habits, or the nation to which they belong. The *organization* of their religion, however, is a very important factor. A highly organized church, with power, wealth and prestige, develops selfishness, ignorance and poverty. A free church, with little organization, property, or power, develops independence, education and prosperity. The curse of Spain was the power and wealth of its churches; while the rise of England was due to the simplicity and poverty of the English faiths. This illustrates why I am opposed to church endowments, paid secretaries, and too much organization.

EDUCATION AND GOVERNMENT

It is true that heads were cut off in England as in Spain. Even the man who translated the Bible into English was burned at the stake. English history has as many black spots as has Spanish history. London should be as ashamed of its Tower as Madrid should be of its prisons. However, there is this difference. The common people of England finally won in their struggle for religious freedom, popular education and social justice. This has not taken place in Spain, even up to the writing of this book. The Spanish civil war, starting in 1936, is largely a fight backed by the rich churches and other property owners on one side; and backed by poor people with misled leaders on the other. England has had its revolutions; it has seemed at times as if London would go the way that Madrid has gone; but in the end England always "muddled through" and became a better and bigger nation.

Anyone who has visited Hyde Park, London, readily understands another reason. Hyde Park and similar places have been a safety valve for England. The government of England has never tied down these safety valves as did the government of Spain in years past. Even after the socialists came into control of Spain, they were as intolerant as were the preceding monarchists. In England the spirit of freedom extended to education as well as to religion. In England people were given an opportunity to succeed. Encouragement was given to scientific research, foreign commerce, and colonization. While the Spanish authorities short-sightedly devoted their energies to maintaining the status quo, the English government encouraged discussion, adventure, and world development. Censorship in England has been almost unknown; while in Spain it was a fundamental law of the land. There was never any regimentation of industry in England. That country was the last nation to adopt a protective tariff. The monarchs of Spain long ago tried the principles of "planned economy"; while England has depended upon "rugged individualism" for its security and growth.

ACTION AND REACTION

Among England's great men was Sir Isaac Newton. Among Sir Isaac Newton's writings will be found great emphasis upon the Law of Action and Reaction. Newton first applied this in connection with his studies of astronomy, physics and chemistry. It was soon evident to him, however, that this famous Law of Action and Reaction applies to nations as well as to materials. Suppression breeds explosions; while freedom develops loyalty. Dictatorships breed ignorance; while general education develops security. In Spain the common people fought to destroy the upper classes and their property; but in England they fought only for opportunity to compete with the upper classes and become a part of them. The English never made the mistake of trying to *force reform or unduly hasten it*. The English motto has been "Be content to follow God, don't try to run ahead of

Him." The English have always believed in Jesus' command "Love thy neighbor as thyself"; but the English have remembered that this was Jesus' *second* commandment. The first commandment was "Obey the Lord thy God."

I cannot too strongly emphasize the relative effect of religion and education in reforming the two countries which we are discussing. Even more important, however, are the *methods* of reform which the governments of these respective countries adopted. It may be that the kings of Spain and England were equally anxious to help their people. Church leaders of both countries used the same Bible and worshiped the same God. The government of Spain, however, used the methods of force, compulsion, and regimentation; while the government of England directed its energy to extending opportunity for development and profit among all classes. English scientists are noted for their discoveries; English ships are noted for their freedom of trade; while English politics are noted for uncensored speech. No one in England has been fearful of the government, whether he has been at the head of a great industry or a humble workman. Nevertheless, England has encouraged universal suffrage, collective bargaining, and every other worthwhile movement.

REVOLUTION OR COALITION

What has all this to do with the subject of this book? the reader may be asking. It has much to do therewith. The Spanish system of suppression developed a complex of fear and distrust among the people.

They felt that, whatever happened, the government would ultimately be against them. Thus they had little use for the government, under any circumstances. When crises came, the people of Spain were both unprepared and indifferent as to how these crises would be met. The Spaniards did not feel that the government belonged to them, but rather that it belonged to the aristocrats and the established Church.

The English, on the contrary, have always had an entirely different point of view. They struggled among themselves in ordinary times to control the government and to change the government. When, however, a crisis arose in England, all parties quickly got together to protect *their* government. The situation in England, politically, has been largely like the case of the proverbial two Irishmen. Although they were both fighting each other, with bloody noses, they turned vehemently upon a stranger who innocently tried to separate them. Against a third party two Irishmen—even when they have been fighting one another—always unite as bosom friends.

England was terribly wounded by the World War. Millions of her best people were killed; her finest ships were sunk; important industries were wrecked; and she was left staggering under a great debt. ENGLAND WAS THREATENED WITH REVOLUTION DURING THE YEARS IMMEDIATELY FOLLOWING THE WORLD WAR. THERE APPEARED TO BE AN IRREMEDIABLE CONFLICT BETWEEN THE LABOR INTERESTS AND THE LANDED CLASS. The diplomats of every foreign country reported from their London embassies that revolution could not be avoided. These foreign observers were all wrong. The English people loved to struggle within their government, but would never risk destroying their government. Hence, when the crisis came, they turned to *Coalition*. When, however, the crisis in Spain came, in 1936, the Spanish people did not think enough of their government to unite all parties in a common cause. All groups went out to destroy the government. The aristocracy and the Church endeavored to go back to a monarchy; the masses of the people headed straight for communism.

Here lies a great lesson for the American people. In the light of history the United States government is still an experiment. It has been existing less than 160 years as a democracy and only a few years in its present form. Every year a greater proportion, made up from both the rich and the poor of our population, is bent upon replacing the American Constitution with some new form of government. What will the result be? No one knows what the future holds for American democracy. A study of history, however, clearly teaches that the answer depends upon whether our different parties will coalesce in an emergency.

Will party power and prestige willingly be sacrificed for the common good? If not, the United States is destined to go the way of Spain. Then what has happened in Madrid will be repeated in New York, Chicago, St. Louis, San Francisco and New Orleans. On the other hand, if the political parties of the United States will now unselfishly follow the example of England and unitedly form and back a coalition government, the United States may hope for many more years of growth and prosperity. Hence, the title of this book is "Coalition or Chaos?"

II

PROBLEMS CONFRONTING THE UNITED STATES

THE United States is facing many difficulties. The first and most serious is the inherent flaw of the Party System. This does not mean that this system has no advantages. The Party System has many inherent factors which are exceedingly valuable. In normal times the Party System should be the accepted system. Although carrying on a conflict between two political parties leads eventually to a revolution, yet a one-party system of government leads eventually to a dictatorship. Everything in this world has its uses and abuses. The Party System is most important and valuable for normal conditions; but in order for the Party System to survive, it must accept Coalition in emergencies. This is absolutely essential in a country like the United States with four distinct groups: Employers, labor, farmers and a government bureaucracy. The last named group must not be forgotten in view of its tremendously increasing numbers.

The success of democracy depends upon adopting a political system combining the use of the Party System in normal times and the use of Coalition in emergencies. Since 1932 the United States has been facing a crisis. It was first necessary that the various New Deal panaceas be tried. Some of these have proved successful and can be continued under the

Party System; but, with the New Deal, there have developed terrible extravagance, unnecessary government interference, deteriorating forms of relief and other features which can be eliminated or rectified only by a Coalition. Under the Party System each party competes with the other in promising greater expenditures, further aid, and unlimited relief. Such competition in promises leads inevitably to collapse. At such times the stampede can be stopped only by all parties temporarily getting together under a coalition government. Coalition becomes the only foundation upon which confidence can be rebuilt. Under such circumstances Coalition furnishes the only fuel upon which the economic engine will run.

WANT IN THE MIDST OF PLENTY

One of the toughest parts of the problem confronting the United States is the so-called paradox of want in the midst of plenty. When poverty and privation arise from natural causes, people will grin and bear it. They will take their medicine. The sufferings from fire, flood and drought, cause anguish but not social unrest. People patiently bow their heads to punishments which are inflicted, as the saying goes, by the wrath of God. They will not forever submit, however, to hunger, cold, and other miseries which they feel are caused by greed, cruelty and injustice. If it were *want* alone which this country is called upon to endure, there would be little chance for the demagogue and rabble-rouser to inflame our people. What sets afflicted men and women marching and touches the torch to revolution is the realization of the poor that their pauperism is needless. Actual poverty in the very midst of potential abundance,— that, psychologically, is what gives the orator and the agitator the whip with which to flog all classes.

Of course, there are some economists who refuse to grant that there is anything wrong with our economic system. These optimists argue that everything will work out perfectly if only profits are promptly put into new investments. This, so they contend, will increase payrolls without at the same time increasing the volume of consumers' goods which must be absorbed. In a way such optimists are right. It is true that a steady expansion of the capital goods industries would be an immense help in keeping up the buying power of industrial workers and farmers. The hitch is that the relative activities of the consumers' goods industries and capital goods industries get out of step temporarily. When that happens our nation faces an emergency,—and it may be a major one.

SAVING LABOR OR DESTROYING CUSTOMERS?

Few people are fully awake to the further possibilities of labor-saving equipment. Despite all that has been written, despite all the furious discussions of this danger, even now this peculiar monster of Frankenstein is not yet seen in its real rôle. The reason why we are still living in a fool's paradise in this respect is because much of the potential labor-saving machinery is still on the drawing-board, in the experimental shop, or in the testing laboratory. Many humane manufacturers balk at putting in the new machinery. They shrink from the thought of throwing more men and women into the street. For example, we used to take great pride in the automatic screw machine that was almost human, that was the last word in speedy production. Now come expert designers with even faster machinery of a new type. They promise that it will form metal parts as nimbly and swiftly as some superhuman operator might shape them out of dough. If that equipment is ever installed in a big way, be ready to see the unemployment figures take another upward leap.

In recent years, unemployment apparently has changed its status from that of acute attack to chronic condition. There was significance in our first Census of Unemployment. It recognized what we are facing in this country. The *poor* we have always had with us. Are we now going to have always with us the *unemployed*? Is this to be the bitter fruit of our triumphant technology,—that in "saving" laborers we have destroyed customers? Surely that would be the kind of purge which even the most powerful economic system might not survive. In *theory*, when considering the incessant stream of discoveries and inventions, this country ought always to be alive with new industries. In *practice*, although we have a sprinkling of such fresh enterprises, they do not nearly equal our needs. Deplorably, but it seems inevitably, unemployment periodically swells into a genuine emergency.

WHY DEBT IS A POWDER MINE

In previous studies of our economic plight, I have pointed out the way in which debt may become a death's-head at the directors' table. The strange and ominous habit of debt is to compound. Someone hailed compound interest as one of the seven inventions which have reshaped the world. Yes, but that feeling of pride in a great discovery was from the viewpoint of the happy lad who *receives* the compound interest! Less is said about the toiling millions who pay the nation's compound interest; pay in harsher costs of living; pay in the tears of economic hardships, made harder yet by the dragging chains of debt. Mathematicians look at the debt loads under which the country is staggering. They describe the way in which the country's debt—corporate debt for example—grows by compound interest. They shake their heads and say it is the geometric type of growth. This means that even though we comfort ourselves with thinking that the percentage rate may stick around a humble 5%, the absolute weight of dollars is expanding steadily and remorselessly. The burden on the camel's back is increased not one straw at a time, but with an ever-swelling momentum. Finally the back must break.

Meanwhile, consider what is happening to production. Remember that production alone is what can support an enlarging load of industrial debt. Provided only that we could expand output, the physical volume of goods, then there would be hope of coping with the debt situation. *If the flood of merchandise from our factories could be increased also according to the compound interest law,* then it might keep pace with indebtedness. The day might be saved. Physical production, however, is bound within the net of mechanical limitations. Engineers advise us that the most that can be hoped for in production is that it can be made to expand—as the mathematicians say—by *arithmetical* growth. This can have but one meaning. Sooner or later debt overwhelms output. Periodically, America must face such a major emergency.

FIXED PRICES VS. FLEXIBLE PRICES

Modern economists are not content to talk about the general level of commodity prices. Such discussion was all very well in the days of a simpler economy. That crude view of the price structure has been upset by the development of the corporation as the chief unit of business. Our price philosophy has been dislocated still further by the assembling of these great corporate bodies into still more gigantic mergers. The effect of such intergration has been profound, particularly upon the field of commodity prices. According to the modern analysis, prices split into two chief groups. The first group consists of what we may call "*flexible*" prices. These can further be characterized as natural or free prices, which float loosely on the economic stream. With relative freedom they advance and decline in response to the play of bullish and bearish influences. They move in response to the forces of supply and demand. Here we have a survival of free competition. Here is a lingering trace of the old ideal of *laissez faire*. The outstanding example of this group is the pricing of agricultural products. Note well the essential characteristic: Production is determined by the dictates of nature; prices must adjust themselves accordingly.

The second great group of commodities represents *"fixed,"* or administered prices. On goods in this category prices are dictated through the power of monopoly, agreement, or harmony of interests. Expressing the situation harshly, we might charge that the market is rigged. When effective demand or consumers' purchasing power wanes, *instead of cutting prices, the arbiters of the administered price cut output.* They drive a peg into prices, and let the full impact of the recession fall upon the factory. Schedules are curtailed; labor forces are slashed. Then we find the spectacle of one section of our economy at the mercy of *free* prices, while the other sections are enjoying *fixed* prices. Result: Periodic drastic emergencies.

OTHER CHAOTIC EMERGENCIES

The system of modern capitalism with its private profits and losses has several other danger spots. We must recognize these as real points of peril,—if we can trust the investigations of earnest and able critics. Moreover, some of these critics are sincere friends of capitalism. They point out its failings not in anger, but in sorrow. Their aim in such investigations is not to pull down capitalism as an evil institution, but to upbuild it as a good institution. The criticism most worthy of serious attention is the erratic and disorganizing swings in the buying power of money. Everybody clamors for sound money, but critics differ on what makes money sound.

One school of thought is that money should remain constant with respect to some criterion such as metallic weight or the number of dollars. The other school of thought condemns a dollar that stretches and shrinks with respects to its purchasing power. To this second group of thinkers, the only sound dollar is one that, year in and year out, will buy an unchanging quantity of goods and services. Furthermore, some of the ablest students of practical economics state that lack of a stable currency, in this sense of constancy of buying power, lies at the root of ninety per cent of the emergencies which confront this country,— and also the world.

When you set out at any time to find what is wrong with the system of private profit and loss you can quickly discover plenty to criticize. For example, there can be very little doubt that absentee ownership is one of the biggest holes in the skimmer. Anybody who has ever gone through the throes of a big proxy fight does not need to be told that the thousand-headed owner of American business—the collective stockholder—is no longer master in his own house. What is everybody's business is nobody's business. Nowhere is this truer than in the case of the stockholder who is derelict in his duty of exercising *in fact* the responsibilities which he carries *in theory*. Here is potential emergency.

CONTAGION OF ALIEN DISEASES

Some time ago a keen diagnostician displayed a map of the world. Those countries which enjoyed the blessing of genuine freedom of the press, freedom of speech, and freedom of thought,—the map-maker left such countries white. Those countries in which all those and other freedoms had been strangled in the grip of dictatorship he marked in black. It is shocking to see how authoritarianism had spread over the face of the globe. The world was congratulating itself that the Dark Ages were a thing of the past. Such a map as this, however, raises the foreboding thought that the black night of tyranny again is dropping down upon the earth.

Geography in hand, run over the roster of the world's nations. Where can you find any country which is not either torn by internal chaos, or else fears that it will be attacked by the aggression of invaders? In the opening chapter we glanced at some of the horrors in Spain. That country is not alone in its agonies. Russia is drenched with its purging. Roumania and others of the Little Entente nations struggle amidst acute upheavals. Disturbing dispatches continually come out of Egypt and the Near East. India is seething. China and Japan threw off one kind of barbarism only to fall into the death grapple of another kind. Even Palestine has changed from Holy Land to Hell.

Almost without exception, every country is enmeshed in one form or another of the underlying struggle between the Tyranny Twins—Communism and Fascism. Originally these ideologies were at opposite extremes. Communism was socialism imposed by violence. Fascism was capitalism imposed by violence. At first glance, the one common element was violence. Otherwise, Communism and Fascism were poles apart. In a circle, however, the ends finally bend around until they meet. Something of the kind seems to have happened with Left and Right. Both are dictatorships. Each carries a menace which can engulf the United States in a supreme emergency. Hence the great importance of Coalition in such emergencies.

COALITION A MIDDLE WAY OUT OF EMERGENCY

Sometimes you see placed about a building various devices for combating fire. Railroad passenger cars are now equipped with a glass case in which are an ax and other tools. On such a glass case or on such pieces of fire-fighting equipment will be a warning notice. It reads: *For Emergency Use Only*. That same caution should be marked on any plan of coalition government. The coalition cure should never be adopted until the situation has developed unmistakably into a real emergency. I do not preach coalition as in any sense a normal design for living. The coalition cure should be administered only for the duration of the emergency. After the emergency has been conquered and has passed, then the coalition cure should be discontinued. *We should fight as vigorously for avoidance of Coalition in normal times as we fight for the adoption of Coalition in abnormal times*. With this all-important qualification we can look to coalition in the proper time and place as a method which is completely democratic.

Democracy goes deeper than a mere mechanical counting of the noses and blindly abiding by the results of the count. The essence of true Democracy is not this mechanical split into a majority and minority. It is not so much a split as a merger. Moreover, it is a merger, or a voluntary cooperation, not merely of major and minor,—but of right and left, of industrial and agricultural, of employer and labor, and of citizen and government. When we visualize Democracy in this broader sense, we see it not as a mechanism of voting, but as an organism of cooperation. This is why we can plead the cause of Coalition as an unexcelled method of moderation. It offers the middle way out of the emergencies which periodically threaten our nation from every direction. Some of these menaces we have listed in this chapter.

III

IS THE PARTY SYSTEM CONSTITUTIONAL?

At various times in the history of the United States it is popular to lay all troubles onto the Constitution or onto the Supreme Court. At one period the Supreme Court is too liberal; while at another period it is too conservative. The Constitution is made "the bad boy," while the Supreme Court is given the whipping. Often this is done to take the people's mind off the troubles caused by bad Congressional legislation. When a law does not work, the Supreme Court is blamed; while the Supreme Court may blame it on the Constitution. One party is extolling the Constitution, while the opposing is deriding the Constitution. This conflict was very severe in 1937 when President Franklin D. Roosevelt was said to be trying to "pack" the Supreme Court. The Republican and other conservative interests talked as if such an event would be suicidal to Democracy. Did they forget that the Supreme Court had been "packed" by the conservatives for many years?

Like Christianity, the United States Constitution has never been tried, except during the very early days of our country's history. The Party System in connection with the election of President and Vice-President is absolutely contrary to the spirit, if not to the letter, of the Constitution of the United States.

The Constitution assumed that the selection of a
President and Vice-President is a professional task
which should be attempted only by those qualified
for the purpose. The Constitution provides that the
voters of a state should decide whom they want as
selectors and electors of their President and Vice-
President. It was never contemplated that party
politics would be considered in the choice of such
men. The plan was that our President and Vice-
President should be chosen on their merits and according to their principles by *electors* who were to
meet and make selection on this basis. The writers
of the Constitution never dreamed that these electors
would be mere figureheads or that any candidates
or parties would dominate in the election of the government's heads.

CHECKS AND BALANCES

Our Party System has entirely departed from this
Constitutional method. It has been suggested that
at any time a presidential election could have been
thrown out as unconstitutional by the Supreme Court.
It has even been hinted by some alarmists that a
Supreme Court of the future will throw out, as unconstitutional, an election in which their party is
defeated. The very fact that the Constitution does
not mention political parties, or in any way refer to
the present machinery used in an election, shows that
a fundamental principle of the Constitution is being
ignored. I go further and say that if democracy
breaks down in the United States, it will—in part—

be due to the fact that this basic principle has been cast aside.

We hear complaints at times that some one of the three basic departments of the government is overstepping. There have been years when the offender has been the Legislative Department; at other times it has been the Executive Department; and doubtless there have been times when it has been the Judicial Department. Certainly, federal courts have been too arbitrary in many instances in placing the importance of property ahead of the importance of men and women. When I was discussing our Constitution with a great English lawyer, he emphasized that the idea of having these three departments as "checks and balances" is America's great contribution to Democracy. Yet there are many times when these checks and balances are not allowed to work. Why is this? A study of the situation shows that the failure may be due to the casting aside of the electoral system which the Constitution planned to be used. It may even be said that whenever the structure of the Constitution has failed, the failure has been due to the crumbling of this foundation.

THE ROOTS OF PARTY GOVERNMENT

The founders of American democracy were the writers of the United States Constitution. They never dreamed that politics would become the business that it has become today, comparable only to the business of religion. The founders of our country were as innocent as were the founders of Christianity, who never envisaged the churches of today with their property, endowments and large payrolls. The writers of the Constitution provided that, once in four years, the people would elect a group of men who, in turn, would elect a President and Vice-President. It never occurred to Thomas Jefferson and his associates that great political parties would be built up, with millions of dollars to spend and thousands of employees to support. The plan assumed by the writers of our Constitution was fundamentally sound.

What corporation could successfully compete in industry, commerce, or merchandising if the stockholders were divided constantly into two competing parties, each endeavoring to undermine the other? For a corporation to succeed it must have a continuity of management. To have the entire board of directors changed once in four years, or even once in eight years, would be very destructive. The only reason why the United States survives under such procedure is because of the nation's natural resources and the government's power of arbitrary taxation. When the natural resources begin to fail the government of the United States must then compete with foreign governments where this constant change of policy does not occur. The United States must even now compete with governments like Russia, Italy, Japan and Germany, operated by dictatorships, where all conflicting parties have been eliminated or welded into one party. Surely the English system of having no Constitution whatsoever is better than the American system of having a Constitution and absolutely ignoring its fundamental principle.

PLOTTINGS OF PARTY LEADERS

The plotting of party leaders between elections is highly detrimental to the welfare of the United States. There is very little thought by these party leaders of what is best for the country as a whole. The simple fact is that those who are "in" are plotting to remain, while those who are "out" are plotting to return. It is a cold-blooded business with them all. This applies not only to the national leaders, but to those in charge of congressional districts, county organizations and even the city wards. Each of these small neighborhoods has two political leaders, one for each party, both craving for support. One of these men always has a job and the other always is out of a job. There is *one* job, but *two* men are always scrambling and plotting for it in every neighborhood. Neither of these men has any special interest in the country's welfare. Neither knows much about economics, history, or good government. As for foreign affairs, both are blind and ignorant.

No one can intelligently consider the Party System without recognizing that these ignorant, unprincipled, and selfish ward-heelers are the foundations of both parties. These men are the roots of the Party System; they are the ones who secure the votes for the party leaders. This sad fact further emphasizes how the fundamental principles of our Constitution have been turned upside down and inside out by ignoring the electoral college. Instead of building our Democracy on the electoral college, made up of the nation's most able and unselfish men, we are letting it be built upon these ward-heelers who have no knowledge of government, but are merely hunting jobs for themselves. This bad situation is even intensified by dickerings and trades and talk of promised jobs, which take place in the notorious "smoke-filled rooms" of state and national party conventions.

PARTY SYSTEM PLATFORMS

It has been said that the platform of a political party may well be compared to the platform of a street car;—that is, it is of use only for "getting aboard." It really is a disgrace both to our government and our voters that party platforms have become mere ornaments in connection with a national election. Not more than one-tenth of one per cent of the voters ever read the platform of one party,— not to mention the platforms of both parties. It is true that the Constitution did not provide for party platforms, and hence it may be wise to ignore them. If, however, they are to be used, the Party System itself should be thoroughly overhauled and revised. The important point to realize, however, is that voters are not prepared to decide fundamental policies as to industry, commerce, foreign trade, and international relations. These are very technical subjects. As an Englishman once said to me: "If you don't like your doctor, discharge him and employ another; but don't attempt to prescribe for yourself or cut out your own appendix."

Again let it be emphasized: The Constitution provides that the voters should select a group of men in whom they have confidence and that these men should form an electoral college to select the captain of the ship of state. The plottings of the Party System for the presidential candidates and platforms were never contemplated. It is bad enough to have these plottings at the various state and national conventions which elect the Senators and Representatives. Under the present system, however, they extend to the presidential campaign as well as to the congressional elections. I am not here criticizing congressional elections or even the use of the Party System in connection therewith. The founders of the American government may have contemplated the use of the Party System in electing congressmen. It is certain, however, their plan contemplated that the three governmental departments should be built up in three different ways. The Executive Department should be selected by the electoral college; the Legislative Department by the people direct; while the Judicial Department would be strictly appointive, subject to the approval of the Senate.

CONSTITUTIONAL AND COALITIONAL

It is strange these two words sound so closely alike! Yet it would not be unreasonable to expect that they are derived from the same roots. For providing the country with an Executive Department surely a coalition form of government was visualized. For providing the country with a Judiciary Department the appointive principle was believed to be best. It is quite possible that the party system was assumed to be more practical for selecting the Legislative Department,—that is, the members of the House of Representatives and, indirectly, the Senate of the

United States. (In this connection it should be mentioned that most students of government have been convinced that the United States took a backward step politically when it amended the Constitution as to the election of senators.)

In a previous chapter it was suggested that a coalition government should be used only in emergencies, but let us now consider another possibility. Would it be practical to use at all times the Party System in the election of Congressmen, but resort to an honest coalition system in electing the President and Executive Department? This surely would give the country the "checks and balances" which it so greatly needs. Some people are always in a great hurry for legislation. They believe that people can be reformed by force. This group is partly responsible both for our legislative mistakes and for the severe reactions which have taken place as a result of the mistaken legislation. Every voter realizes that passing a law will not make water run uphill or prevent teeth from decaying. Congress can pass laws *appropriating money* to pump water uphill or to distribute aspirin to the population. Neither of these things, however, accomplishes the desired result.

THE SHIP "CONSTITUTION"

Readers who have visited the capitol at Washington have seen a large picture of the ship Constitution which hangs on one of the walls. I have always been interested in the ship because this picture was painted by a friend of mine living at Rockport, Massachusetts, Gilbert T. Margeson. He has painted many remarkable marine pictures, but I think this one of the Constitution is his masterpiece. When I once asked what inspired him while doing this work, he stated that his inspiration was the things for which the good ship Constitution stands and was named. In painting this ship he visualized it as a bulwark for Democracy, a protector of freedom, and an opportunity for progress. If one will study the painting, he will see that these fundamental factors stand out most clearly. Let me relate how the name "Constitution" came to be selected.

On the one-hundredth anniversary of the building of the Constitution, I had the pleasure of visiting the ship. It came to Cape Ann, where the painter of the picture was then living. I then read the history of the ship to ascertain the real purpose for which it was built. I found that in the early days of our republic, England, France, Spain and other great nations freely picked upon and harassed our commerce. There then was no such thing as international law. The law of the jungle applied to the seas. Ships flying the flags of strong nations were unmolested, but ships flying the flag of "that weak American democracy" received little consideration. Our able diplomats, such as Benjamin Franklin, secured somewhat decent treatment by England and some other leading nations; but these diplomats could not get these nations to eliminate an organized group of pirates who operated off the Barbary Coast. In fact, it was generally believed that these pirates were being financed by individuals in these countries.

When, however, the English and French governments, notwithstanding their great navies, reported to the American people that they were unable to stop the piracy off the Barbary Coast, the Americans courageously replied: "All right, but with the help of God we will try ourselves to stop this piracy." Thereupon the young American government built two sailing vessels which it fitted with homemade cannon and manned with brave seamen from Gloucester and other New England ports. These early Americans, although poor and weak, believed that the only enduring security rested with courage. They visualized the American Democracy as synonomous with their Constitution as written by James Madison and adopted by the Convention of 1787. Hence they named the larger of these sailing ships the "Constitution," the other the "Constellation."

The American government in those days, over 100 years ago, was made up of realists and not theorists. The leaders understood that for the country to succeed, the written constitution must be backed up by a brave and unselfish people. They even felt that the success or failure of their little American democracy would ultimately be determined by whether or not it had the hardihood to sink privateers which were molesting its commerce. Hence, the ship Constitution and its sister ship were sailed across the Atlantic Ocean to eliminate pirates off the Barbary Coast, whom the great navies of England and France dared not to offend. Yet later this same nation of ours permitted the Japanese to sink one of its government gunboats, the *Panay*, because we "feared becoming involved in foreign entanglements." I close this chapter with the thought that instead of merely writing notes it

might have been far better for our government to
have built a great superb aircraft carrier with a fleet
of super-bombing planes, to have named it "Coalition," and to have anchored it in the harbor of
Tokyo.

IV

POLITICAL EXPEDIENCY VS.
FITNESS FOR OFFICE

WHEN in England, I have met and worked with leaders of the coalition government who at intervals have directed English policy in a most troubled world. Surely England has had troubles, being located in the very center of a turbulent sea with London within a few bombing hours of Moscow, Berlin and Rome. Still, the British government has kept lighted the flame of Democracy, while Stalin, Hitler, Mussolini and other dictators are desperately trying to blow it out. Any traveler who impartially studies the subject is convinced that England's strength is her ability to unite in a coalition government whenever the need arises. Notwithstanding that England is a democracy, her people are far more unitedly behind the government than are the people of Russia, Germany or Italy behind their dictators. As I have visited the House of Commons, I have heard different party leaders criticize one another, some in fun and some seriously; but when a crucial moment comes, all parties are predominantly united.

The coalition government of England has another advantage in its ability to secure more able men than our party government secures in the United States. When a coalition government comes into power, it is not necessary to reward the winning party with all kinds of jobs for all kinds of people. Men can be selected by the English for executive positions according to their fitness and training. To a large extent this means continuing in office men who successfully and unselfishly perform their duties. This not only secures a continuity of policy, but adds to the respect for the government both at home and abroad. Compare this with the American system, where the politicians use sectional appeal as movie directors use sex appeal. There is no "favorite son" fetish in connection with a coalition government. The demands of sections, groups, and parties are secondary to fitness, honesty, and courage.

ROOSEVELT'S ADVISERS

The people of the United States owe much to the Roosevelt Administration. It accomplished in a few years what would have taken a generation or two under ordinary conditions. The hatred and abuse which wealthy people have given Franklin D. Roosevelt is both unjust and unwise. It is generally agreed, however, even among his own party leaders, that he made a mistake in selecting his sympathetic and "economic" assistants. He should not have given such authority to lecturers, professors and social workers who had never had any real experience as either employers or wage workers. Each reformer had his pet panacea for economic difficulties. They seemed united in one thing only, namely, in undermining confidence. These inexperienced surgeons were allowed to operate on Uncle Sam's body. Someone said: "They tapped it here; they prodded it there; and they tested it somewhere else to get social and unsocial reactions." None seemed to realize that the mistakes of these professors must be paid for, at the expense of more than one hundred million innocent people.

Probably there is no one factor of government so important as taxation. In a later chapter I shall deal with taxes. Suffice it here to say: Whether the existing system of taxation is right or wrong, it is the product of centuries of study and experimentation. Furthermore, the present agricultural and industrial system, which employs all the nation's people, operates on the existing tax system. I do not say that "money is a very delicate flower which needs most carefully nurturing"; but I am convinced that changing the tax system can either provide with employment or throw out of employment millions of people. Despite this principle and without any regard for past experience, the Roosevelt Administration unwisely tinkered with the most important problem of taxation. When the reformers did not do harm enough, labor union officials were taken on as advisers on matters concerning which they knew little. It certainly seems to outsiders that these things were done for political purposes and not for the good of the nation. The concrete question is: Can this mistaken policy now be corrected except through a coalition government?

THE OHIO TRADITION

Although Roosevelt apparently picked some of his advisers in the wrong way, it would ill become any political party to cast a stone at him for this reason. If sometimes he used unwise standards in drafting his leaders, what shall we say about the way in which political parties pick *their* candidates? We can only say—and this is one of the weightiest charges against the Party System—that the parties do not pick their candidates on the basis of fitness for office. Rather the supreme test is political expediency. To appreciate this point you have only to listen to the discussions that range around the names of potential presidential candidates during the election year. Rarely if ever is there any serious debate on a candidate's intrinsic qualifications. In the dictionary of the party politician the one word is "availability," which means the candidate's ability to pull votes. The grave issue in selecting even a chief executive of the nation is discussed in such terms, for example, as the "Ohio tradition." Think of appealing to a fetish that candidates from this state or any particular state thereby are endowed with peculiar fitness for office.

The geographic test is also illustrated in the "New York tradition." This would have us believe a New York governor is almost *ex officio* the right kind of man for President. Now it is undeniable that a governorship can be considered as training for the presidency. We have no quarrel with tradition on this score. In the lingo of the politicians, however, what counts is not the man's training from such an office, but his "availability." Party strategists reckon not virtues nor vices,—but votes!

BUILD-UP AND GROOMING

Both in the race for the nomination and in the battle for the election, the presidential aspirant is handled by party press agents in much the same spirit as they work to create reputation for a motion picture star or tooth paste. All who reflect upon the real significance of the presidency should be disgusted and disquieted to see him treated in this manner. Probably the operation of the Party System will never be able to get away from the necessity of this synthetic creation, this elaborate "building up" of the nominee, this cynical "grooming" of the candidate. It seems to be implicit in the Party System that political expediency and opportunism shall be exaggerated. Likewise the system appears to play down fundamental fitness for office and genuine capacity for true service. This is one of the big reasons why politics in public esteem has become so smeared with ill repute. If the politicians do not like to be a joke, let them first correct the Party System. It underlies a large part of political vice and crime.

You ask how this ailment can be alleviated by occasional applications of a coalition regime for limited periods in times of emergency. This goes straight to the prior question of what we mean by fitness for office. In the modern development of society, administrative and executive office is inseparably connected with economics,—*applied* economics. This does not mean that an administration should be composed of business men. Perhaps the best way to put the point is to insist that fitness for high office calls for a generous measure of training, experience, and character needed for a genuine success in legitimate business and employment. We may or may not take pride in the fact that the United States has become dominantly a business nation. Nevertheless, it does seem foolish not to apply to our major political officials some of the fitness tests that would be used in choosing the leaders of a great business organization.

PURGE OF OUR PRESIDENTS

In connection with the choosing of our presidents, it is appropriate to devote a little thought to our wastefulness in neglecting to use the talents of our ex-presidents and other former party leaders. In the red lands of communism, when the dictator is swept by a fit of jitters, he starts a purge. From the outside it looks as if these periodic purges were depriving the afflicted nation of the services of some of its ablest officials. Of the United States we can speak from closer contact. In this country we know for a sure fact that when we let our chief executive go, he takes with him some almost priceless assets of knowledge, training and experience. It is true that our ex-presidents do not remain idle. Usually they are not the type that retires. They are welcomed by private enterprise. They are drafted into various kinds of humanitarian service. Such a job, however, is not the kind for which they are best fitted for distinguished activity. All told, the nation has spent millions of dollars to elect these men. It has spent hundreds of millions of dollars to train them. Why not capitalize this investment?

In his executive capacity a president gets an incomparable training. As one of our presidents once remarked: "The chief executive stands at a crossroad not only of the nation but of the world. He is at a supreme nerve-center of the currents of finance, industry, labor, agriculture, distribution, commerce, and social conditions. The education thus forced upon him cannot be matched in any other post." Similar conclusions apply to other leading officials in a national administration. This brings up the question of "career men," those members of the government's personnel who have not entered public life for a temporary office-holder's tenure. Rather their status is that of one who makes public service a profession. It is widely recognized that such men can give a devotion and character of service which are unexcelled. Why cannot all officials be career men if we can arrange to save them from the purge of the Party System?

WASHINGTON EDUCATION

When working with the government during the World War, I learned what every government worker knows: Washington is a surpassing source of data. Facts and figures are there obtainable readily on nearly every conceivable subject. People in other localities have commented on the mass of reports which come out of Washington in the form of census volumes and the bulletins of the other departments. Let me state that the information which comes out of this city is but a small fraction of the knowledge which remains there in storage. I have often advised research men in other localities who were starting on some survey or project: "Look to Washington first; after you have looked there you may not need to look further." If a subject is known by anybody in the United States, or even in the world, the chances are that it is known by somebody at the Capital. Not only are the files stuffed with exhibits, but there is usually some humble expert glad to give you the desired information personally. For courtesy and helpfulness, our federal staff is unexcelled. This is the magnificent university in which our Presidents and their associates get their schooling.

Also while at Washington I came to appreciate that the leaders of an administration have unrivaled opportunities for making contacts. These are personal meetings with key people in strategic positions all over the land and in every branch of activity. There are few of our nation's progressive directors of industry and other activities who do not find their way to Washington fairly frequently. According to the rantings of the agitators, all who go to the Capitol go there to lobby. This is no more true than most of the other tirades of the demagogue. I make the statement that the vast majority of both business men and labor leaders stand ready at all times to meet Washington in a spirit of cooperation and coalition. They visit Washington to give, as well as to get. To officials of the right type such opportunity for contacts is an education in itself.

PARTY SYSTEM AT LEAST A SCREEN

Although the Party System is often used as a smoke-screen to cover up considerable trickery and villainy, it acts as a screen in another sense. In choosing its candidates for national office, a party is compelled to screen out at least those seekers of office who are grossly unfit. Cynics may sneer at the big holes in the screen; but still it does its work in a broad way. Even when Presidential and other candidates are selected primarily for political expediency, and not fitness for office, the choice must reasonably be intelligent on both counts. The public may love to be humbugged, but even the most brazen party must give some weight to fitness. The truth of this is borne out by examination of our Presidents over the years. Surely, compared with the characters of some of our bankers and industrialists we must concede that our political parties have somehow managed to do a fairly creditable job of picking the men at the top.

This affords added reason why Uncle Sam is a poor business man in discarding his intelligent but defeated party leaders. Because of the screening process, as applied by the party in choosing its standard-bearers, these ex-administrators are picked men. We need their services not alone during their tenure of office, but after that term has expired. If the truth were published, the high officialdom of Washington would be plastered with HELP WANTED signs. Notoriously the chief executive is overworked. The job of President of the United States has steadily become more burdensome. If a job analysis—such as a private business organization employs—were made of the functions required of our President, it would be shown that some of his burdens should be lifted and allotted elsewhere.

WHERE TO PUT OUR EX-EXECUTIVES

In hunting for some worthy and efficient position to which an ex-president or party leader can be called, one of the most promising suggestions is in connection with Coalition. The King of England has no power in normal times but is of vast service in emergencies. This opportunity for extending an ex-president's term of service to the nation would be conferred automatically or—so to speak—ex officio. The thought, however, is that the purpose of such a procedure would not be to confer honor upon the ex-president. Such a call to emergency service would not be in the nature of a medal or diploma. Rather, the nation needs the man, instead of the man needing attention from the nation. In the foregoing sections, we have developed the many reasons why a man cannot serve as chief executive of this country without acquiring a unique and unrivaled education. We want the continued benefits of that education. Coalition provides the way.

At present every one in Congress represents some regional constituency. New England senators and representatives are supposed to fight for New England; Western senators and representatives to fight for the West; Southerners to fight for the South. Some students of government tell us that is an evil heirloom from the days when this country was an assortment of unrelated and disconnected areas. Certainly in no immediate future, and perhaps never, will it be possible to reform our congressmen and make their attitude nation-wide instead of local. However, one or more ex-presidents and distinguished party leaders taking service in emergencies could reasonably be called upon to represent every section. A Coalition government would naturally do this.

V

DO WE NEED NEW PARTIES?

DURING the World War when I was Director of Information and Education of the Labor Administration, I had the honor of working closely with President Woodrow Wilson. I also helped the Labor Department in connection with its appropriations from Congress, representing it at the various committee hearings. In connection with this work I came in frequent contact with Cordell Hull. He was a member of the House of Representatives at that time and had much influence upon appropriations. Readers who were active in those days realize the tremendous change which took place in Washington after the Harding victory. Most of the prominent Democrats were defeated for office; appropriations were slashed mercilessly; and the only thing left for us to do was to pack our trunks and return home.

My father had brought me up to "keep my fences mended." He would urge me to call on people once in awhile when I did not want something of them. Therefore in the winter of 1920-21, although I was leaving Washington for good, it seemed only fair for me to take time to call upon my old Democratic friends, even though they had been defeated. I therefore devoted two or three days to these calls. Among those upon whom I called was Cordell Hull. I found him at the head office of the National Democratic Committee, of which he had reluctantly assumed the chairmanship. It was a very small office. He was trying to write a letter on the typewriter by the "hunt and peck" method, as the Committee had no funds to supply him with a stenographer. Said he:

"My friends tell me that the Democratic Party is done for. They claim that we won the last elections only by a fluke. One thing is certain: Unless I can get fifty dollars for overdue rent, I fear that the National Headquarters will immediately be closed."

In this opinion the leading political writers of that day concurred.

POLITICAL FORECASTS DANGEROUS

This talk with Cordell Hull just followed Harding's election. If anyone had foretold to Mr. Hull and his associates that in about ten years the Democrats would sweep the country by an unprecedented vote, and that he himself would head the Cabinet as Secretary of State, he would have had such a prophet put in an asylum. Yet this is exactly what took place. It means that political forecasts are very uncertain and cannot be depended upon. This thought could further be illustrated by reference to the tremendous enthusiasm of the Republican Party in the days of Coolidge. Anyone who might then have forecast that in ten years the Republican Party would win only two of our forty-eight states would likewise have been declared insane. The collapse of the Republican Party was as much a surprise as the rebirth of the Democratic Party.

These are important facts to keep in mind because so many defeatists at times believe that the Republican Party should give up its name and go out of business. It may be that a realignment of parties is advisable. On account of Southern prejudices the term "Republican" should perhaps be eliminated. Many suggestions of a new name have been made. Perhaps the most acceptable is the name "Constitutional Party." The idea is that there should be a realignment by the conservative Republicans and the conservative Democrats uniting in one party. This would leave the liberal Republicans and liberal Democrats in another party. The liberals would further hope that the radical parties would join with them. Such a realignment may come about; but it is not the purpose of this book to recommend it. The English people for generations have been lined up in this proposed manner; nevertheless, it has been necessary for them to resort to coalition in emergencies. It is the use of Coalition at critical times which this book is urging, rather than a mere realignment of parties. Furthermore, it is very probable that the Republican Party can some day come back and sweep the country even without a change of name.

COMMUNISM AND FASCISM

Many thinking people are much disturbed at times with the rising tides of Communism and Fascism. It appears that the nations of Europe and Asia are lining up with one group or the other. This even applies to the countries of South and Central America. Many believe that if another World War should soon take place it would be between these two groups. Personally, I question this, believing that such a war would be between the democratic countries of England, France and the United States on one side, and the fascist countries of Italy, Germany and Japan on the other side. Russia is very likely to remain out of the fight, with the hope that both sides will become so exhausted that she can step in at the end and dictate the terms of peace. Whatever the future holds, however, it is vital that the waves of neither Communism nor Fascism should engulf the United States.

The question then arises as to what shall we do about Communism and Fascism? The very fact that these systems are growing so steadily in power is evidence that they both have something good to present to the people. Among the sound elements of these systems we can mention for example the following. Both Communism and Fascism, at least in their claims, are operated for the benefit of the "have nots." The leaders appeal particularly to the lowly and dispossessed masses. If such a foundation is sought sincerely, it is a worthy goal. In the next place, both of these systems are essentially more efficient than democracy, at least over a certain period of time. If these radical systems have various good features, they cannot be exterminated by persecuting or ignoring. Furthermore it would be very risky for either the Democratic or Republican parties, directly or indirectly, to align themselves with either of these radical elements. A coalition, however, adopting the good and ruthlessly casting out the bad, could safely do this. In fact many believe that only through a coalition of the two major parties can the country be saved from a tidal wave of either Communism or Fascism. It may even be that unless such a Coalition takes place, accepting the good features of these radical groups, the United States may suffer an internal conflict as has Spain.

NATIONALISM VS. NATIONALISM

Europe has been swept by so-called nationalism. This has resulted in reducing the standard of living, annihilating foreign trade, and making enmities with neighboring countries. This nationalistic policy, as customarily followed, is both uneconomic and unchristian. It is bound to lead either to war or bankruptcy. It is the most dangerous feature of the situation in Europe. Nationalism is even winning the people of England and her colonies. This is evidenced by the "Buy British" campaign which has been fostered in Great Britain. The increasing persecution of the Jewish race is a feature of this nationalistic insanity. The boycott of Japanese goods in the United States could easily extend to the boycotting of all foreign goods. Nationalism, as set up and practised in Europe, must not be allowed to scourge the United States. It is too dangerous and has too far-reaching consequences. A very thin veil exists between boycott and warfare.

Yet it must be realized that there is something inherently instinctive in the nationalistic movement. Self-preservation is the first law of nature, and self-propagation is the second law of nature. Man has always fought for his family and his group, realizing that, as Kipling said, "the strength of the wolf is the pack." Therefore, the only way to head off an unreasonable nationalism is to give the people a rational nationalism. This means that the people of the United States should be given some practical means, in an emergency, of expressing their nationalistic instincts. Is not Coalition such a way? Is not Coalition a synonym for a sane nationalism? By the major parties uniting for a time in a coalition government, this instinctive nationalistic feeling can be capitalized for the benefit of the nation and the welfare of all. Let us direct nationalism along constructive channels and thus prevent erosion. Let it be our slave rather than our master. Nationalism is too dangerous a force either to play with or to ignore.

EXPENSE OF SWITCHING

Once when I was traveling from New York to Webber College, at Babson Park, Florida, the train was delayed for some time at Jacksonville. This seemed entirely unnecessary, as all component parts of the train were in the station. When I spoke of the delay to a train official, he explained it was due to "switching." He further said that not only a large amount of time is thus wasted, but also a large amount of money. "If train switching could be eliminated," he said, "the railroads of the country would immediately be on a paying basis; bond holders would be getting their interest; and no increase in railroad rates would be necessary." Surely this is something for both investors and shippers to consider. If so, the railroads certainly need a coalition railroad government for uniting the transportation of this country. It rather appears that only through such a coalition management would wasteful competition be eliminated and more efficient operation be developed.

Let us look at the problem of "switching" from another point of view. An old saying is: "Do not swap horses when crossing a stream." This homely philosophy means that it is very dangerous to make radical changes in times of trouble. When one attempts to change from one horse to another in the middle of a stream he is likely to fall between the two horses and be drowned. Naturally this argument is used by an administration in office to hold its position. Therefore such an administration naturally refuses to collaborate with the opposition, believing that the voters' fear of "switching" would prolong its power. This, however, is a very selfish line of defense if not an untenable defense. Certainly it is a plea good for only a limited period. The inefficiency of "switching" can be eliminated, as in the case of railroads, only through consolidating. This means that the disadvantages of "switching" from one political party to another can be avoided only through some practical form of Coalition. True progress comes from building on the foundations already existing and using the good material of all political parties.

DANGERS OF INFLATION

The American people are very temperamental. The American people are very quick to forget.

After a few days of rainy weather, they forget that the sun ever shines; while, after a few days of pleasant weather, they forget it ever rains. This human trait may be one cause for the business cycle, with its corresponding periods of prosperity and depression. As there can be no valleys without hills, so there can be no business depressions without preceding periods of abnormal prosperity. This attitude on the part of the American public is especially noticeable in connection with the subject of inflation. During every business depression a large group of people have urged the printing of currency, increasing the government debt, and other inflationary measures as a solution of the country's problems. During these depressions the inflationists come very near forcing the country over the brink into the abyss. It has seemed that only a return to better business, at an opportune time, has saved the country from being ruined by these misguided jugglers of the dollar. As soon as good times return, nothing more is heard about inflation until bad times come again.

Whether inflation will be in the limelight as you read this book cannot now be foretold. It can be said with certainty, however, that the whole world has been headed toward inflation since 1933. This applies especially to the United States. The rise in wages, the failure to balance the budget, and the creeping of politics into our banking system are bringing an inflationary era closer each day. This book does not need to comment on the great dangers of an inflationary movement. Radical inflation means disaster for every group. No sure hedge against it is known. Even although one of the major political parties violently opposes inflation, the other party can win votes by advocating it. Inflation is presented as a sort of Santa Claus. No political party ever succeeded by talking against Santa Claus. Radical inflation and its terrible aftermath can be checked only by the major parties entering into a coalition until the dangers of inflation blow over.

STUDY THE FARM VOTE

Every student who studies the situation must recognize the importance of agriculture. The farms of the country are the fountain source of the nation's wealth. Other sources, such as the forests and mines, temporarily provide wealth; but their productivity is limited. The farming sections of our nation provide a continuous source of income, *and the only permanent source of income*. The prosperity enjoyed in the cities is born on the farm. This is irrespective of the farms' producing the food of the nation upon which the very life of the nation depends. The most important agricultural product is not wheat, corn, cotton and hogs. The most important crop consists of the children born and brought up on our farms. It seems to need the training which one gets on a farm to develop independence, initiative, industry and courage. These are the qualities which made America. Almost every successful captain of industry, operating from a great skyscraper in New York, Chicago or some other large city, was born on a farm.

Congress is justified in helping the farmers; but it should be sure that real help is being extended. Children are not helped merely by being given what they want. It is not fair to the efficient farmers for the government to help all inefficient farmers. Besides, children brought up by a shiftless, poverty-stricken farm family add nothing to the manhood and womanhood of America. Therefore, for a farm to be worthy of help, it must not need help in the long run. All that intelligent farmers ask, therefore, is that they have no handicaps and are given the same treatment as to tariffs, subsidies and other legislation, that is afforded to the industrial sections. Yet each political party is sorely tempted to cater to the farmers' vote, irrespective of what is best for the farmer and the nation in the long run. The farmers' vote can be used as a trap by which the one who baits it finally is caught. Nevertheless, it is very risky for either of the major parties to tell the farmers the truth. Only by these major parties coalescing for awhile in one national government can justice be assured both to farmers and the tax-payers.

WHAT ABOUT THE LABOR VOTE?

The same line of reasoning applies to the labor vote. Labor has its just claims, but organized labor is not the only form of labor. It is very wrong for a government to disregard four fifths of the population because one fifth is organized. Yet this organized minority is very troublesome. Each political party knows it is dangerous to ignore a minority. One political party is tempted to outbid the other in offering all kinds of useless panaceas just to get votes. As a result, the political parties compete one against another as to which can offer the most attractive bait, irrespective of the dangerous hooks which this bait contains. This is likewise true of the relief problem which is confronting the country. It is very dangerous for either political party to cut off relief. Yet the leaders of all parties know that it must be stopped, sooner or later.

A coalition government, however, would be in a position to consider the questions of prices, profits, labor, wages, hours, relief and allied subjects on their merits. If new laws are necessary for the welfare of any group, such legislation could then quickly be enacted. If on the other hand, certain existing legislation should be repealed, such repeal could then take place without hearing either of the major political parties or their leaders. This is the way England has solved its pressing problems to the satisfaction of both employers and wage workers. England has long had votes by women, old age pensions, unemployment insurance, and other forms of progressive and New Deal legislation. Collective bargaining is recognized universally in England. England has a strong Labor Party which, at one time, had full control of the government. Even this Labor Party saw that it had the bull by the tail. It knew that it would be destroyed whether it hung on or let go! This Labor Party was very glad to turn its power over to coalition government. It seems as if England's experience in this connection would influence both the conservative and the radical elements in America to unite, for a time at least, in a similar manner. Let us always remember that a policy which is suicide for any individual party may spell salvation to both if inaugurated by a coalition government.

IMPORTANCE OF RESEARCH

Truly to help labor, Coalition must be backed up by research. The possibilities of service and invention have been merely scratched. Yet any political party when in control at Washington finds it more popular to legislate for price regulation than for increased production. They say that to convince voters of the need of more goods—when there appears to be a surplus—requires too much "education." Here office seekers of both parties follow the line of least resistance and blame all things to prices and wages. They know that both farmers and city people lack the courage to let prices take a natural course. Administrations especially like to get after large corporations, which, they contend, are depressing or boosting prices, according to which charge best suits their political audience.

Furthermore, politicians fear political reactions from localities or industries and even foreign countries which might suffer from the development of new industries and new processes. This is true notwithstanding that the only solution to the unemployment problem is through increased production, new industries and scientific research. Over forty per cent of the American people need better homes, new furniture and better education. It is often the fear of political leaders of temporarily harming certain existent real estate and lagging manufacturing centers that is preventing our citizens from making and enjoying these needed improvements.

VI

PARTY LEADERS AND COALITION

POLITICAL folk ways, like any other folk ways, die hard! We have had the two-party system in American politics ingrained into us until it has long since become a part of our national consciousness. Occasionally there has been a flare-up. For a short space a third party would flash meteorlike across the nation's political skies. The Populist party, the Greenback party, the Progressive party— there have been more than a few down the years. But after a brief, often somewhat hysterical, career, these movements invariably have vanished. We then settled back to the good old days of two parties, of torchlight parades,—of viewing-with-alarm or pointing-with-pride—all depending upon whether our party was "in" or "out" of power.

The World War marked the end of that golden political age. When Woodrow Wilson mobilized the nation for war he did not think and act as a President elected by the Democratic party. He called upon *all* leaders in the national life—business men, labor chieftains, technical experts, professional men—regardless of party, to meet the emergency which the war created. The response was a *coalition* response, —a coalition of the spirits and energies of men in a common cause. Party lines, which were blurred by the war, have never since resumed their previous

clarity of separation. The only trouble has been that
the American people have failed to realize that the
Party System then received a very severe blow.

OLD PARTIES AND OLD ISSUES

There was a resurgence of old-time partisan politics under President Harding. It was a natural reaction to the war. We all wanted to get back to the
"normalcy" which Harding epitomized by his easy-
going, *laissez faire* Administration. It, however, was
a false reassurance which the nation received under
Mr. Harding's Administration and under his Republican successors, Presidents Coolidge and Hoover.
Both old parties and old issues were becoming ill.
They needed a surgical operation.

We did not stop to realize that those characteristics
which ever since the Civil War had separated the two
major parties were no longer real issues. The tariff
had ceased to be a partisan issue representing two
separate philosophies of free trade and protection.
The issue of state rights versus a strong centralized
Federal control no longer was the sole property of
either Democrats or Republicans. Even before the
depression-governed political conventions of 1932,
one could no longer find any basic differences in the
major platforms of both parties.

Nations have moved on and new folk ways of
government have come into being throughout the
world. We have stream-lined our methods of producing and distributing. We have set up efficiency
as a yardstick in all our ways of living;—all, that is,
except in our methods of governing ourselves in the

United States. This is a machine age,—an age of magnificent improvements in the technological processes by which men live more abundantly, more successfully, more happily. Has our political machinery become too obsolete to stand the strain of emergencies?

UNITED STATES AS BAD AS CHINA

Yet we have been content in our country to ignore all these improvements in so far as applying them to our democratic processes of government is concerned. The United States leads the world in terms of inventive genius, in terms of efficient industrialism, in terms of modernity in economics and social programs. The United States, however, is little better than China in its lassitude and torpor regarding its political institutions. A crisis shows up the flaws. I know this is an extreme statement to make, but I make it deliberately and thoughtfully.

I will go even further. I say that today the ridiculous political divisions by which our nation is divided into states, counties, cities, townships and the like are worse than inefficient. They are criminal. Some of our states and most of our counties are frankly nothing but rackets. Too often they are in the hands of racketeers just as much as narcotics, white slavery, horse racing, or "numbers" are rackets in the hands of racketeers. No sane person who will pause long enough to examine some of these time-honored methods of government can fail to come to any other conclusion. For example, at least 80 per cent of the counties in the United States could be abolished. Their costly and practically useless machinery—so heavy a burden upon the taxpayer—might be eliminated to the benefit of all of us.

I realize that to suggest we abolish our state governments is a rank heresy to many. I do not go to that limit, even though some of our states are woeful examples of abuse and a complete contradiction of their original purposes. When they were established in the young days of the Republic it was done merely to aid the political party then in office. There are sentimental reasons for keeping state lines. But since the original purposes for which municipalities, counties and states were first set up have in considerable measure vanished, we should no longer allow these institutions to be the plunder-pockets of politicians. We surely should eliminate them rather than have them continue as the loot-centers of racketeers who call themselves Republicans or Democrats.

SCRAP COUNTIES IF NECESSARY

Huey Long lived long enough to demonstrate how these so-called "democratic institutions of the people" can be converted into a personal machine by a strong, intelligent and unscrupulous leader. What happened in Louisiana can happen—it has happened in a lesser way already—elsewhere. Therefore, since these methods of governing no longer serve their intended purposes, I am no radical or iconoclast when I speak as follows: *The people should face the facts and remedy the evils by reconstructing our government from top to bottom.* Just as the boundary lines of any corporation, any labor union, any group method of accomplishing a common objective are constantly being modified to meet new conditions, so should the lines of our county and other political units be changed.

I said that the states need not be scrapped. But stop and think of how costly, in terms of heavy state taxes, is the burden we assume in these local institutions. A governor can appoint a few judges, can keep an eye on the various state bodies,—but at the most it does not demand a great deal. The local legislatures and city councils grind out thousands of statutes, one community contradicting another, making the flow of commerce and of communication increasingly difficult. We have forty-eight little principalities trying to function as one nation—and achieving a maximum in confusion and chaos. We govern ourselves,—but at what a cost!

So—just as the English people have long since done with their monarchy—let us keep these sentimental backgrounds, but let us keep them as backgrounds. King George is important to the English people; but important in those intangible terms of character and tradition for which the Crown stands in the eyes of British subjects. I, too, have similar loyalties. I am a citizen of Massachusetts; my forebears long ago gave me a proud heritage in a little seacoast corner of that state. I *am* proud of these staunch New England traditions. But because of them I do not think that the city of Gloucester, where I was born, nor the county of Essex, in which Gloucester lies, nor the Commonwealth of Massachusetts are functioning efficiently as governing units.

THE REAL DIFFICULTY

In saying this, permit me to put my finger directly upon the major difficulty in bringing about the changes which would lift us out of this slough of political confusion. I state what is necessary to give our American democracy a real chance to function successfully in a world of efficient dictatorships of the Left and the Right. The difficulty is this: *Political leaders, both local and national, depend for their continued power upon all this local machinery.* The network is too intricately bound up with the careers of every man in political life from a town officer to a United States Senator. The only way the nation can free itself from this mess is through a Coalition government. It is a critical task which no *one* party can accomplish.

I have talked with men in public life about this problem,—men holding high positions. One man, whose probity is of the highest and whom I personally admire—a member of the United States Senate—said to me recently:

"Babson, of course you are right. We *ought* to move toward a Coalition form of government. I believe in it. But the party leaders of neither side will agree to any such compromise. They will not agree because of the local politicians in their respective districts and because of the machines which are necessary to elect men to office and keep them there."

The Senator may be right; but if so, the party leaders are selfish, cowardly and unpatriotic.

LEARN FROM EUROPEAN EVENTS

So far this chapter has considered only the domestic aspects of the need for a coalition government. But the greater need is reflected in the developments that are taking place outside the boundaries of our nation. When in Europe I have had an opportunity of learning at first hand what is going on there. We are a generation behind every government abroad in terms of our methods of running national affairs. I am not here discussing the relative merits of the *kind* of government which Hitler is operating in Germany, or Stalin is operating in Russia, or the British people have in Great Britain. I believe in Democracy and not in Dictatorship.

At the same time I do *not* believe in the kind of muddled, stupid and dishonest democracy we have in this country. I *do* believe in the efficiency, realism and technique which I found in Europe. In short, we must make our democracy work in terms of today, in terms of Twentieth Century values. If we do not, it may mean the end of democratic institutions, the collapse of our ideals and the failure of the kind of government which our founding fathers established. We will then be ready for the Man on Horseback who is riding ruthlessly over the map of Europe today.

WHAT VOTERS WANT

What do I propose to our political leaders? How can they help at this time? I can answer that succinctly and constructively. The voters want the po-

litical leaders of both parties to meet at an early date
and lay plans for a joint Presidential convention of
Republicans and Democrats. This convention should
take the place of the two separate political conventions which are ordinarily scheduled. It should nomi-
nate a man for President who will represent the best
choice of the best men of both parties. It should do
this in accordance with the plan outlined in the Constitution of the United States.

This convention should cut through party lines
completely. It should ignore the local pullings and
haulings of small-bore politicans. It should pay no
heed to those content to keep their home fences up
and whose every action is dominated by these cross-
currents of motives. It should ignore those who give
no attention to the nation's welfare or to the larger
purposes of government. It is these local machines
which will offer the strongest opposition to Coalition.
They know what will happen to them. So, if the
party leaders—the men of broad-gauge perceptions
and ideals in both parties—would unite in a call for
a Coalition Convention, Democracy will have gone a
great way toward winning its battle.

The United Front is a slogan to conjure with all
over the world. We need it here in the United States.
We need it desperately and urgently. Look back at
the two last political conventions. What mockeries
they were,—what reflections upon the intelligence of
our voters. Nomination by ballyhoo, selection of a
Presidential candidate by noise-making gadgets in
the hands of ward-heelers. See-what-the-boys-in-
the-back-room-will-have type of politicians. Yet I
am sure that this situation cannot be remedied by

starting in the local districts—or by getting this or that Congressman or Senator to argue for reform. These party leaders can and will act only if they can act in concert. No one of them, or no small group of them, will get out on a limb alone and thereby endanger their own political futures.

A CHALLENGE TO ALL

If, however, Franklin Roosevelt and his advisers *mean* the political idealism which they are so fond of declaiming; if Herbert Hoover, John Hamilton, Alf Landon, Senator Vandenberg and other Republicans mean what *they* say, then it should be entirely feasible to get this movement started. I refer to a movement for a Coalition Convention by efforts of those who are at the top. I know this can be done because I have canvassed the sentiment of some of the best men at the nation's Capital. They all agree that the world situation demands some sort of coalition government in the United States—or else! That "or else" is a grim shadow that hangs over the democracies of the world. It is a shadow that looms as either Fascist or Communist, depending upon whether you look toward Germany, Italy or Japan on the one hand, or toward Russia on the other.

VII

GOVERNMENT PYRAMIDING CAUSES
TAX BURDENS

UNDER any system of parties, patronage, and spoils, the cost of government pyramids to fantastic proportions. It lays upon the nation an appalling load of *costs* and *taxes* and *debts*. Already this pyramid has exceeded the margin of social safety. Let us glance at the cost of government if put on a pay-as-you-go basis instead of running into debt. If we paid on the nail instead of trying to postpone the fiscal doomsday, cost of government would load upon the backs of our people a burden of about thirty cents out of every dollar they earn. The average family is compelled to toil and slave, to support its government, about four months out of every year! Moreover, that burden is still growing. The gambling mania lures its victims to try to *get* something for nothing. The tax racket forces people to *give* something for nothing,—or at least to give a lot for a little. This chapter is devoted to taxation. Nevertheless, I remind you that taxation is but one of the many death sentences which are imposed upon a nation when it refuses to meet emergency situations with first-aid treatment, namely, with a coalition government. I shall deal with our tax problem frankly, but only as a single specific example of how, in times of storm, we face coalition or chaos.

Remember that everything said here of taxation applies with equal sharpness to unemployment, inefficiency, chicanery, and every other villainy of the Party System. This does not mean that we should junk any system for good and all. It does not mean that we should set a coalition government forever upon the throne. In fact, to install coalition in perpetuity would be to inaugurate a dictatorship. America does not crave a dictatorship of a decayed coalition which has outlived the emergency which brought it into power. Therefore any discussion of taxes should be angled not from the normal costs of governmental operation, but rather from the abnormal heights to which these costs have pyramided. According to the old saying: "There are only two sure things in this world, death and taxes." To these twin certainties, a triplet can now be added. The third sure thing is that *taxes are* death when they soar above a certain normal line. Then, but not until then, comes a clear call for Coalition.

WHO IS GUILTY?

Woodrow Wilson fell heir to a world war. Herbert Hoover fell heir to a world depression. Franklin D. Roosevelt was the legatee of a world cataclysm which was filled with the fury both of military and economic forces. The "Great Democrat And Pacifist" could not keep us out of war. The "Great Engineer" could not shield us from the avalanche of world depression. The "Great Humanitarian"—and I sincerely believe Roosevelt to be this both in name and in heart—could not sweep back the tides of un-

employment, super-taxation, underlying class conflict, and other emergency phenomena. To lay these
ugly offspring on the doorsteps of the White House
alone is unfair and unintelligent; Franklin Roosevelt
fell heir to the end result, the final build-up of tidal
forces of almost cosmic scale.

These tides have been crawling onward through
generations. For critics to try to put 100% respon-
sibility upon one individual or one party is senseless.
It is on a par with the justice and intelligence of the
old Roman custom of beheading the bearer of bad
tidings. Both the Republicans and the Democrats
are responsible for our high tax burdens. Jointly they
should be held accountable to remedy the situation.
Jointly they should shoulder the job of finding the
way out. I say *jointly*, not severally. Jointly means
in coalition. Therefore the only practical step, the
only rational step, is not to waste words and thoughts
scheming to fix the tax guilt. Pin the blame on history. The important and immediate assignment now
is to survey this crushing impost as to its abnormality,—then work out a coalition solution to the
problem.

THE BAD NEWS

Now draw up to the adding machine and look at
the annual operating costs of government in this
country in 1938. Our federal government piles up
annual running costs of some five billion dollars, not
including the interest charges and payment on the
principal of tax-exempt government bonds. In addition, the states—forty-eight of them—call for *an-*

nual operating costs of two and a half billion dollars annually. Finally come the local boys, the cities and counties, and they need an *annual* total of about four and a half billion dollars, just trying to get along. Now crank up your adding machine. The grand total, if your addition checks with mine, is twelve billion dollars *per year* to keep our government in business. That is a stupendous sum on any man's cash register. If "The Bad News" were gradually declining, we might be cheerful. If it were even holding steady, there might be hope. The trend, however, shows that government costs are neither lessening nor leveling, but are continually advancing toward higher levels. Always the vital thing in a study of statistics is the direction of change. In our governmental cost and tax statistics the direction of change is ominous. The record points straight to abnormality and emergency,—and the eventual necessity of coalition control.

Take down from the shelf your history. At different stages of our national development a varying percentage of the people's income has been plundered by the rapacious taxgatherer. In 1850 this budgetary bandit despoiled our population of a mere 5% of their annual earnings. As late as 1890, his "take" was only 7% of the family exchequer. The racket held at that small-time percentage until the economic aftermath of the World War. Then, in 1921 for example, we find our U. S. citizenry paid taxes to the tune of 16% of their annual income. On the basis that world economy became abnormal after the World War we can class as super-taxation any such mulcting of the taxpayer. In the modern period, taxes eat into our people's incomes by percentages ranging from about 15% to nearly 20%. (We are talking now of direct taxes: hidden taxes make a bad matter worse.) Expenditures of Government from Washington to Wilson (1789-1913) a total of 124 years, was $24,521,843,000. Expenditures of the Roosevelt Administration as estimated by the President—(actual 1934 and estimated 1935 and 1936) total of 3 years—was $24,206,533,000.

SOAKING THE POOR

Taxes are of two broad kinds. Open or direct taxes may soak the rich; but hidden taxes soak the poor. When I call these indirect taxes "hidden," I mean that they are hidden deeply. They are not lightly covered with leaves, but buried far below the reach of official statistics. Hidden taxes can be disclosed only by the "geo-physics" or dowser's rod of special research. So we shall have to forego statistics and scan merely the evidence only too familiar to every business man, every good housewife, and every economist. One way to drag hidden taxes into the open would be to print the "bad news" (i.e. the amount of the tax) on every price tag. Then the hidden taxes would erupt to the surface with the violence of a volcano. What would be the effect politically? It would be little short of devastating. Probably no party in power could hope to survive the rebellion that would result from the awakening of the public to the atrocities of taxation.

All the time, beneath the surface, these hidden taxes are draining every consumer like an internal hemorrhage. Every day we thus are taxed around the clock, from the hidden-taxed toothbrush which we use on arising to the hidden-taxed slippers into which we shuffle off to our hidden-taxed bed. Every year we are taxed around the calendar, from the hidden-taxed flower bulbs which we plant in the spring to the hidden-taxed electric bulbs which we hang on our Christmas tree. Every life is riddled with hidden taxes, all the way from infants' wear to burial garments. Our fathers loved to say: "All that I have, I owe to some good woman." What our children will have to say is: "All that I have, I *owe* to some bad government,—and it is howling for payment." It would be a comedy if it stopped short of a tragedy. The tragic element is that because of hidden taxes an overwhelming load is laid upon the back of those least able to withstand it.

Hidden taxes have become the "watered stock" of the poor, diluting still further the poor's pitiful share in the national heritage. It is no joke to see the predatory tax collectors insanely plundering those of the upper brackets. It is the most successful known way to undermine enterprise and sink the whole nation into the miseries of a deteriorating economy. But I can stand the spectacle of fiscal terrorism against the top-flight taxpayers. After all, most of the big boys know how to take care of themselves by recapturing some of the loot. What upsets me is to see the frightfulness of the hidden-tax butchery of the poor. It is reminiscent of the atrocity stories coming out of Russia. The Soviet coat of arms is a Hammer, which I assume to symbolize Industry, and a Sickle, presumably a tribute to Agriculture. If I may offer a free suggestion to the Comintern, why not the Hammer as the sign of the Skull-Cracker and the Sickle as the sign of the Throat-Cutter?

It would be well for Russia to add to her emblem one more feature, namely, a Star; ultimately even the Soviet will learn that without some spiritual significance no flag is anything but a rag. But Russia is not the only country that takes the comrades for a ride. In the U. S. S. R. the Cheka practised the physical liquidation of their comrades by the firing squad. In the U. S. A. we effect the economic liquidation of our comrades by the taxing squad. We work, not with the bullets but with bills—the bills for hidden taxes. The American method is more democratic, more humane, more Christian. But even our bloodless pillaging and purging of the populace is not very good democracy, or humanitarianism, or Christianity.

OUR CHAMBER OF HORRORS

Modern merchandise is protected by transparent wrappings. At the same time it is swathed by another transparent wrapper of invisible taxes. The loaf of bread which the trusting housewife buys is loaded with fifty-three taxes which she pays. In a bottle of milk of magnesia the price is swollen by ninety-four manufacturing and seventy-eight retail taxes. One manufacturer in the pharmaceutical industry tried to explore the taxes on his business; his auditors counted a total of three hundred and seventy-eight different taxes which the company was compelled to pay. Each telephone in service is estimated to represent $6.76 in annual taxes; about one-sixth of the cost of electric light service is chargeable to taxes. Those are some of the data disclosed by the Institute Of Distribution. The old expression "free as air" must be abandoned; because the filling station that provides "free air" for your tires pays a sales tax or its equivalent on the air compressor and a tax on the electricity which runs the compressor.

Hotels are said to pay at least fourteen different kinds of taxes. The following are estimates for some of the indirect taxes borne by low and moderate-income workers not owning real estate: On insurance, 3%; on food 7%; on clothing 8%; on fuel and light, recreation, and miscellaneous items, 10%; on automobile transportation 21%; on shelter 25%. In 1927 the Curtis Publishing Company filed fourteen tax returns with Federal, state and local governments of the United States. It cost $850 to prepare them. In 1937 the same company was compelled to file about 44,500 tax returns, the cost of preparing which was $21,000. Yet both in 1927 and in 1937 only one tax return was required for the vast business which it does in the Dominion of Canada.

This Chamber of Horrors of taxation could be prolonged without end. Such abominable levies are economic vermin and parasites infesting every class of society from bottom to top. Our industrial and commercial structure is riddled and honeycombed with taxes. The situation has progressively become worse. It is an emergency. Yet no one political party can hope to attack and liquidate the evils of taxation because such liquidation would drain temporarily the hog troughs at which the party feeds. To combat and conquer the taxation crisis requires the combined resources of Coalition. Such coalition is one kind of "power pool" which merits the approval and support of all responsible citizens. Let us revise the old line. Let us make it read, "Now is the time for all good men to come to the aid of—not the party—but the union of parties." In such union is the strength to strike down an intolerable plague. Coalition alone has the might to put its axes into our taxes.

BRUTAL TO BUSINESS MEN

In times of emergency employment waits upon revival of business activity. Particularly pressing is the need of reawakening new ventures in the capital goods industries. All this forward surge of enterprise depends upon the mainspring of confidence among both business men and wage workers. Business men especially are always ready to sing a hymn of hate against the hamstringing of business by savage taxation. The voice of business is loudest against the evils of capital gains levies and the undistributed profits tax. No piece of legislation, it is said, makes fewer friends and more enemies than the "confiscation" of undistributed profits,—for these are viewed by management as reserves and "seed corn" against the lean years. Such taxation, whatever the academic arguments, surely puts horror in the hearts of the industrial leaders whose confidence and courage are the first steps in creating employment. Business men are no fools: They know full well that social needs exist and must be met. They would be the last to want to set back the clock of civilization, drop the standards of living. They realize—none better—that the government must have sources of revenue. What they ask is: That the methods of raising the revenue do not demolish the business structure from which that revenue is derived.

Executives who must look a payroll in the eye every week recommend that government revenue should be obtained by businesslike procedure. Specifically their advice is to reform taxation by broadening the base. Instead of sticking more taxes on a loaf of bread—already it is plastered with some fifty-three taxes—they counsel the government to spread taxation over more bread-winners. Tough on the bread-winner? Yes, but even under coalition control, any governmental drive to cut taxes needs public support. It needs widespread "tax consciousness," every shoe on every foot in the nation painfully pinched. Probably that is the first step which a coalition government would take toward a more rational taxation,—broadening the base.

COALITION REFORM OF TAX CHAOS

When advocating a coalition government to deal with emergency conditions, I have been asked to state how such a body might deal with the crisis of taxation. Here is the proposed outline of such a program:

Broaden The Income Tax Base.
Pare Down Nuisance Taxes.
Reduce Capital Gains Assessments.

Eliminate Tax-Exempt Securities.
Tax Government Employees.
Remove The Undistributed Profits Tax.
Set Aside Social Security Funds.
Clamp Down On Special Local Taxes.
Lower Real Estate Taxes.
Cut Public Spending.

That is an ambitious program; but it cuts to the core of our tangle of emergency conditions. More important, it leads to the development of confidence from which every citizen will benefit. It should however be plain that far-reaching plans of this kind can be executed only through the emergency powers of Coalition.

ANOTHER EXAMPLE

Here is a practical example of how an emergency Coalition could take steps to improve business, expand government revenues, and thus permit the reduction of tax rates. I call this the Quota Plan. While I was engaged in war-time work for the government, the nation was forced to grapple with two successive problems. First, was the problem of mobilizing labor into military service. Second, after the Armistice, was the opposite problem of demobilizing the service men back into private employment. In this drive to return men to industry we worked out plans for assigning to each corporation a quota,—a specified number of men whom the corporation was required to take into its employ. It was the reverse of the war-time draft when we took quotas out of industry.   As it happened, such a peace-time "draft" was not needed; industry picked up, and called for men on its own initiative.

However, the Quota Plan was good.   Years later, during the World Depression, again I advocated this plan as a sound solution of the crisis of unemployment.   I suggested that corporations be permitted to pay their taxes in the form of providing jobs.   Both the government and the great corporations were interested.   Nevertheless, the plan was not put into effect.   Each corporation wanted some other corporation to be the first to take on its assigned quota of employees.   Industry distrusted Government, and Government reciprocated.   I learned a bitter lesson: In times of emergency, in the very hour that confidence and cooperation should rise to new highs they may sink to new lows.   The master key to successful operation of such measures as the Quota Plan is Coalition.

RATIONAL TAXES VS. SUPER-TAXES

I am sure, however, that it is cockeyed strategy to assail rational taxes.   The fanatics and extremists in the camp of the antis are no help to the legitimate reform of taxation.   They are almost as unreasonable and anti-social and dangerous as the Sons of Santa Claus who would have Uncle Sam scatter doles like confetti.   Because I am a liberal, rather than a radical, on the taxation problem, I have often been chided by some of my friends in the "Economy League" movements.   These Rightist pressure groups and agitators sometimes have been guilty of bad timing in their drives. In the midst of profound depression, for example, to start cheering for economy is simply to deepen the gloom. This tends to seal the public's already shut pocketbooks and shrink goverment revenues still further by smacking down on business activity. Surely, when a single political group alone stages a *bearish* raid on spending, it ought at least to pick a time when the public is *bullish*.

All men of goodwill and social vision want to see America blessed with steady progress of the standards of living. By giving everybody in our democracy an opportunity to earn the "abundant life," we protect this democracy against the aggression of alien and hostile systems. Schools, roads, hospitals, armaments, and other public essentials raise private standards of living. Taxpayers are driven so desperate by the bleeding from iniquitous taxation, that they lose their heads as well as their shirts. They would burn down the barn to cremate the rats. Without touching any sound activity of government, there are plenty of ways to nick expenses and mark down the tax rates. Particularly in local government, the potential savings without sacrifice of genuine services are literally legion.

Tear out the ramshackle and cumbersome structure of obsolescence, duplication, corruption, and political barbarism that disgraces much of our local public machinery. By cleaning house in this one area alone, a good efficiency staff could show the taxpayers a precipitate drop in costs and a handsome cut in the tax rates. Everybody knows what ought to be done. Many know how to do it. Then why is it left undone? I will tell you why: Because neither

side cares or dares to mop up the mess alone and un-
aided. Suppose that the Right made a pass at government spending. Every radio on the land would
roar and crackle with the tirades against the heart-
less Tories, Bourbons, economic royalists, and aristo-
cratic anarchists. Yes, the very fact that radio
broadcasting and movie theaters now exist makes
more essential the need of Coalition.

On the other side, what would happen if the gen-
tlemen to left of center started an economy drive?
—if you can imagine such a change of heart. In a
flash, the followers would turn on their former
leaders and patrons and tear them apart. Neither
loyalty, nor party solidarity, nor "ideology," nor
gratitude for favors received, would stand up for one
minute against threats to the job and the lunch box.
Only an emergency merger of Right and Left can
afford or survive the hoisting of the banner of economy,—and then only because the *combination* of
parties commands confidence. And here a word about
confidence. Without minimizing the importance of
confidence in bringing about full employment, let
me say this. Confidence among business men and
investors is sufficient to revive employment in the
heavy goods industries; but more than this is necessary. Confidence among the wageworkers must be
revived before unemployment will be eliminated.
They must believe that their jobs are safe before they
will purchase consumer goods to the extent needed to
keep all workers employed.

ONLY TWO WAYS TO CUT TAXES

This problem of taxation is not something which can be side-stepped or smoothed over by political platforms. Nations are up against not platitudes and pleasantries, but rigorous mathematical conditions. Taxes can be reduced in only two ways:

1. *Taxes can be reduced by cutting expenses.* As to the difficulty of retrenchment, no argument is needed to anybody who ever sweat over the pruning of a business expense sheet or the lopping off of excrescences from a family budget. To expand expenses is as sweet and easy as dropping an eel into an oil tank. To curtail expenses is as tough a job as pulling a hedgehog down a chimney flue by his tail. Keep this in mind also: Slashing the magnificent proportions of a governmental budget is a bitter and thankless task. The story is told of Mr. Henry Ford that sometimes, when poring over the stupendous balance sheets and income and expense statements of the Ford Motor Company, he would take a blotter and cover up most of the figures on the right-hand columns. Thus the various items were not changed in relative *proportion*, but in actual amount they were pulled down to an ordinary human scale where plain "hoss sense" could be applied. Goverment officials might try this Ford psychology.

2. *Taxes can be reduced by improving general business throughout the country.* By thus building up business volumes, values and earnings, the cost of taxation to each individual can legitimately be lessened. This is not the so-called "broadening of the base" of taxation, a matter which I shall discuss

later. Moreover, it is not jacking up the rates, most of which are already at the highest level, which can be borne. The enlargement of government income which flows automatically from the expansion of the nation's business is a blessing alike both to the tax collector and his victims. One of the most beneficient fruits of a period of prosperity is the resulting opportunity of easing the tax burden.

COALITION THE SOLE ANSWER

In dealing with each of these two tax-reduction methods, it is plain that Coalition alone is competent to cope with the stubborn difficulties involved. For example, take the first tax-lowering plan,—the trimming down of the government's running expenses. Like the private budget problem, the public budget problem instantly brings up this delicate question. *Whose* head will be cut off? *Whose* toes will be stepped upon? The government expense item for relief costs is a representative case. Repeatedly, government officials have been appealed to by the public with the plea: "We cannot let people starve! We cannot see them destitute of housing and clothing! We cannot put property values above human values!" Always there has been but one response. However, there can be no doubt that great efficiencies might be developed in the administration of relief. Even the most ardent champion of human values must admit that much of the relief load could fairly and properly be borne by families, friends, and local resources.

Can you imagine, however, what would happen to

any political party which puts into execution, or
even advocates, a really firm-handed and realistic
dealing with the relief problem? Such a move on the
part of any political group would instantaneously
create a situation made-to-order for its political foes.
Cannot you already see with your mind's eye the
crocodile tears which would stream from every opposition editorial writer in the country? Cannot you
hear in your mind's ear the sob-brethren on the radio
broadcast hook-ups? For any one party—either
Democratic or Republican—to lay hands on the national budget and really slash it would be to write
its political obituary. Retrenchment, curtailment,
economy, efficiency,—these moves can be made only
by a coalition government drafted for such emergency service. Why? Because "you cannot indict
a nation,"—and neither can you punish and over-
throw a coalition government. Such a control, although temporary in its tenure, is unconquerable,
impregnable, and unassailable for the limited period
while it is in power. Its strength is in proportion to
the variety and complexity of the interests which it
represents.

COALITION CAN IMPROVE IMPAIRED BUSINESS

Finally, turn to the second of the two ways in
which taxes can be reduced. This opportunity
comes only as the result of business improvement,
with resulting enlargement of government revenue.
Here is a motto which might well stand on the desk
of every high official and might well be stuck under

the hatband of every influential citizen. The motto reads:

"Only public confidence will swell public receipts."

Let us develop this idea specifically. What is meant by "normal" business? This does not mean stagnant business or that our economic activity shall remain at a dead level. In this still unfolding land of America it is truly "normal" that business shall continually grow as the country increases in wealth, population, and enterprise. Activity is excessive only when the volume of business rises above this natural upward slope of normal growth.

On the other hand, business becomes subnormal when the volume thereof drops below this steady upward pitch. We would not suggest coalition control if business was not below normal. Politicians should pray for business to stick to that golden mean and develop moderately; for that is the condition which makes the Party System workable. Once the tides of our economic affairs sag down into a valley, beneath the line of normal growth, then politics should step out and the coalition step in. Government revenues are increased and tax-reduction possibilities are created only when business grows right. Business grows right only when the whole country feels right. The whole country feels right—when menaced by emergency conditions—only under coalition control.

VIII

COALITION AND PROSPERITY

THE only earning power which a government really has is through taxation. When government enters industry, does it add to the wealth of the country as a whole? Not only could such work usually be done more efficiently through private channels, but whenever the government does anything itself it may throw many people out of work. The government can build up new things which private capital, for the time being, cannot afford to do. This very fact, however, shows that the government would be doing the task before it is needed. The time may come when people are so imbued with the spirit of Jesus that a socialistic program will be efficient and practical. No such time, however, is now in sight. Many believe there is nothing, from carrying the mails to the building of battleships, that private initiative cannot do better, cheaper, and more efficiently. I hope the time will come when cooperation will take the place of competition. Then we all can work together in the spirit of our Master with the interest of the group as our sole goal.

The government's system of bookkeeping should be honest and not misleading. The government may be justified in owning water powers and coal reserves; but the main reason therefor would be to prevent waste and see that these natural resources are enjoyed fairly by all. When building and operating, however, the government should present its financial statements in an honest manner. The usual method of government financing is dishonest. Continually putting out more bonds to pay interest charges is like a corporation fooling its investors by paying dividends with borrowed money. Such a policy must be stopped or else disaster will be the end. This is not an appeal for the protection of any one group of investors or business men. Because public utility operators paid outrageous prices for properties which they purchased,—that is no reason why a President should not demand lower electric rates. I simply say that the government should work honestly and keep its books honestly.

EXPENDITURES FOR RELIEF

Every sane man—whether a conservative or a radical, an employer or a wageworker—must realize that the present system of relief cannot continue indefinitely. It is foolish to think that the government can always borrow money to hire men and women to do unproductive work. Any such policy is simply an attempt to ignore the multiplication table and the Ten Commandments. Any such attempt is sure to end in a collapse. The law of reward and punishment is as fundamental as the law of supply and demand or the law of gravitation. Every one is entitled to an opportunity to work, but not necessarily to get the job which he or she would like. The establishment of a policy, however, that "no one shall under any conditions want for food in the United

States" is utterly unsound, both economically and ethically. Just as the fear of pain is necessary to make us take care of our bodies, so the fear of starvation is necessary to make us work for our nation.

Economic history shows that this country suffered previous business depressions far worse than anything witnessed from 1930 to 1936. Yet no one starved during those depressions, even though much hardship was endured. At those previous times it was recognized that the first duty of a family was to take care of its unfortunate or unemployed members. Those who were unable to work, or would not work and had no sustaining relatives, went to the poorhouse. Statistics show that *very few* went to the poorhouse! The then government position that the unemployed must be supported by other members of the family had a very salutary effect. This automatically made each family a police force to see that the idle members returned to work whenever the opportunity offered, irrespective of whether or not the work was to their liking. To return to such a system is the only solution of the relief problem. For any major party now to advocate this, however, would be very risky. Only a coalition government can get us back on the right track.

STANDARDS OF LIVING

Voters should understand that government has been of little help in lifting the nation's standard of living. The people of the United States enjoy a higher standard of living because of scientists working in laboratories,—not because of politicians legislating in Congress. The improved standards of living enjoyed by Americans has been due to scientific discoveries and improved labor-saving inventions. Both government officials and labor leaders have taken credit for something which they had small part in bringing about. Nevertheless, politicians delight in persecuting the very industrial leaders who are responsible for these improved standards of living. The radio and its broadcasting have become a very potent factor in this misapprehension. The moving picture industry has also aided. In this connection let it be said that were it not for radio broadcasting, the dictators of Europe would never have secured their present extraordinary and arbitrary power.

The political power which one individual can secure through radio broadcasting is something to consider seriously. So long as this situation continues, America, as well as the rest of the world, is sitting on a keg of dynamite. To give free radio time to one because he happens to be in power is very dangerous; while to attempt to censor radio broadcasting is equally dangerous. The only solution to the problem is through a coalition control of radio broadcasting. Certainly a coalition government is necessary in order to muster courage to tell the voters the truth about living standards. The tendency to give either politicians or labor leaders the credit for America's high standards of living is misleading. The main reason why America leads the rest of the world in living standards is because of the money, intelligence and energy which have been spent by corporations to develop new processes, new industries, and new machinery. When any congressman or government official persecutes, for temporary advantage, these corporations or the "sixty families" controlling them, a grave injustice is done to the American people.

WHAT ABOUT WAGES?

Everyone would like to have a continual increase of wages among all groups of workers. Next to the productivity of farms, it is essential to increase the purchasing power of those industrially employed. The purchasing power of the masses always should be kept in balance with the savings of capital. Otherwise, the economic ship will overturn. The ultimate strength of every nation depends on a more equal division of the wealth of that nation among all its worthy people. Therefore, the protection of all who "have" depends on securing more for those who "have not." Those who "have" must give up, although those who "have not" must wake up. Increased income to stick, however, must come about through increased production. There is more to divide only as more is produced. This is something which should be taught, even if a coalition government is necessary to put this message across.

One serious feature of the labor problem is the attempt of all highly organized groups to have practically the same wage. It must be recognized that with changed conditions certain groups must suffer. This is being illustrated among the coal miners and the railway workers. Any attempt to relieve these or similar groups by legislation or labor unions, without recognizing this fundamental difficulty, is an injustice to the workers themselves. Another illustration is a comparison of the automobile industry with the building industry. The automobile workers have devised new machinery and methods which have greatly increased their production. They are therefore entitled to higher wages. This, however, is not true of those in the building trades. A painter, for instance, now covers no more wood in an hour than did a painter twenty-five or even fifty years ago. Statistics would probably show that he paints less surface today in an hour than did his grandfather in the same time. Yet the painters expect an increase in wages similar, in percentage, to that secured by more deserving groups. This situation must be recognized and corrected.

LABOR ENTERS POLITICS

Politicians are always afraid of labor leaders. They know that every member of a labor union is a voter —and that fact catches the politician where the hair is short in his efforts as legislator or administrator to deal with labor problems. The rise of organized labor in the United States to a position of political power has been extremely swift since 1935. But even before John L. Lewis and the CIO mushroomed to overnight political importance, labor played a powerful rôle on the political stage of city, state and nation.

Samuel Gompers, for years the head of the American Federation of Labor, followed a very simple and very effective policy. He refused to marshal organized labor under the banner of the Republican party or the Democratic party. He believed that labor should "reward its friends and punish its enemies," regardless of party or political creed. In this way organized labor was able to command the allegiance of many politicians in both parties. They knew that the strength of union labor at the polls might be solidly diverted to their opponents in a local fight—and it did not matter whether that support went to a Republican or a Democrat.

During the Franklin Roosevelt Administration we have seen the emergence of the Lewis-led industrial unions into the direct political field. In New York City, Mayor La Guardia owed his 1937 election in considerable measure to the manner in which the workers united behind him as members of the newly formed American Labor Party. All this, in my opinion, is a dangerous symptom of our times.

EMPLOYMENT PROBLEMS MOST IMPORTANT

It is true that corporations, at times and in certain places, have controlled legislatures and have "owned" governors and mayors. Certain corruptions have flourished in high places, sponsored by the business and financial interests. This is an evil, whether practiced by employers or labor leaders. Wherever it exists, it should be fought by all those who believe in the integrity of our political institutions. Therefore, for the very same reasons for which I have always opposed business controlling our politics and politicians I oppose labor organizations moving in a like direction.

The above dangerous tendency is made possible

under the Party System whereby those men who must stand for election at regular intervals are subject to the influence of an organized minority's votes. They know that their opponents may defeat them if they do not watch their step and play up to every small but well organized minority. Under a Coalition much of this danger would be removed. Then the men who were being held responsible by *all* the people of the nation for the proper administration and legislation of its affairs would be able to act without fear or favor.

Often the most important problems affecting the welfare of the country are employment problems. This may be increasingly true during the twentieth century. Labor is coming of age. The men who run our government will increasingly have to meet and solve problems affecting employment, in which the welfare of all of us will be involved. These problems must be solved. Yet we have only to look back upon the disgraceful exhibition on the part of the Labor Administration in the spring of 1936 to realize how vital is probity on the part of our political leaders.

LABOR ENTITLED TO FULL-TIME WORK

Many believe that Secretary of Labor Perkins—the first woman ever to hold that important post—was guilty of humilating capitulation to "disorganized labor" in connection with the sit-down strikes that marked that period. It took indignant, and in some cases violent, action of the public itself before the Administration modified its policies and ceased to truckle to the outrageous and extremist demands of certain labor agitators. This could not happen under coalition.

From labor's own point of view, a coalition government would be advantageous. Labor is too often made the football of political opportunists in both parties. If the labor tide is rising—as in a period of business improvement—the politicians will curry favor with labor and give it whatever labor asks. On the other hand, labor is in a temporary eclipse during a depression, with a labor surplus clogging the market. Then the opposite is true and labor is unjustly treated. In the long run neither the Harding nor the Perkins policy is helpful to labor. Full-time work with lower prices is much better than intermittent work with high wages. What has happened in the building trades proves this.

What labor really needs is twelve months, all year round, fair and just treatment. It should not be riding high, wide and handsome some of the time, and standing with its hat in hand other times. All this, under a Coalition government, would not be necessary or possible. The problems of labor will never be solved completely. They will always be with us. They are an integral part of our growth as a people. Hence, they should constantly be subject to sympathetic but scientific consideration. Solution lies in the laboratory of human relations, not on the hustings of political parties or in a show of hands. A Coalition would bring the scalpel of the scientist to these problems. There has been too much of partisanship and too little of policy in the handling of our labor problems. As a result all groups have suffered.

IX

WORTH MORE THAN GOLD

I ONCE attended a school debate when the general subject was: "Power." Each of three debaters took a different line of thought. One expounded the physical powers and told what has been accomplished by water power, steam power and electric power. Another debater presented the intellect as the greatest source of power and described what the world owes to the invention of the alphabet, moveable type and literature. The third debater insisted that faith has accomplished the greatest things in this world. He explained the power of confidence, credit, and friendship. The task of the judges was to decide which of these debaters had presented the best case. After long discussion they awarded the prize to the third, who presented confidence as the greatest force in the development of natural resources, industry, and commerce.

My home at Wellesley, Massachusetts, is within a few miles of South Natick, where John Eliot had his famous mission for the Indians. I have always been interested in studying the history of these Indians. They lived in the midst of natural resources. All of the natural wealth which ever existed in New England was there three hundred years ago. There was more virgin timber in the forests, more fish in the sea, while the country then abounded in wild game of all kinds. The land must have been very fertile; the streams were rich in undeveloped power; while an unlimited quantity of sheep, cattle and hogs could have been fed on the meadows. Notwithstanding these natural advantages, it appears that the Indians had lived amongst them for centuries without using them. John Eliot's letters show the Indians had not then even constructed a canoe, nor learned how to preserve fish, nor even made anything in quantities for market. After catching enough fish for immediate needs the Indians "never wet a hook," as Florida fishermen say. As a result, they lived on the fat of the land in the summer; but starved during the winter. After living with these Indians, Eliot concluded it was their distrust of one another that prevented them from working and saving.

HOW INDUSTRY STARTED IN AMERICA

John Eliot did not scold these Indians for what they had not done. Neither did he threaten them by talking about what would happen if they did not do more. John Eliot preached one theme: namely, Faith,—faith in God and faith in one another. It was some time before he began to see any results; but one day he saw some Indians building a canoe. They had never built one before, believing that it would be stolen from them as soon as it was completed. Finally the first canoe was finished and tied to a stump by the side of the Charles River. Probably those Indians laid awake all night wondering whether they would find any canoe in the morning. When the dawn broke, however, the canoe was there. This gave faith to other Indians and soon a small fleet of canoes had been built. This was the beginning of America's great merchant marine.

As I have indicated, the Indians would preserve and store no fish or fowl for winter use, even though it was very abundant during the summer season. The Indians must have known how to do this because they were evaporating salt from the ocean and using it with their food. John Eliot found that the real resaon why they did not preserve and save this food was because of distrust. They felt that it would be stolen or at least would be the cause of riot and massacre within the little village. So they thought it was best for all to try to go through the winter without sufficient food. After John Eliot was well into his work of preaching and teaching, the Indians began to have faith enough to try out their "Apostle's" doctrine. They not only caught enough fish and killed enough fowl to provide for their summer wants, but they dried great quantities on trees and rocks for use in the winter. This was the beginning of America's great packing industry. Perhaps America needs a John Eliot today to revive confidence and speed the wheels of industry.

A STATEMENT THAT HAS ENDURED 2,000 YEARS

Once upon a time a strange man wandered about Jerusalem and the cities of Galilee. He preached a philosophy which was very strange to the people of that day. Some laughed at him; others worshiped him; while the established church crucified him. Among other things, he said:

"If ye have faith as a grain of mustard seed,
ye shall say unto this mountain, 'Remove hence
to yonder place,' and it shall remove. Nothing
shall be impossible unto you."

It was nearly 2,000 years ago that Jesus of Nazareth preached this doctrine. Even though it seemed
strange then, and still seems strange, there must be
something in it, to survive during these nearly 2,000
years. Perhaps it was these words which inspired the
Pilgrims to come to America and carve our great nation out of the rugged hills and dense forests which
they found.

I saw much of Newton D. Baker when he was
Secretary of War under President Wilson. I was
with him one very dark day in 1918 when a cable
arrived from Paris which troubled him greatly. The
cable said that the French were losing confidence in
their commanders and might refuse to cooperate
with General Pershing. After a moment's hesitation,
the Secretary of War turned to me and said:

"Babson, you are interested in business barometers.
Let me give you one which is the result of my years
of experience. It is this: The best barometer of a
nation's future is the ability of the people to
cooperate and to have confidence in their leaders.
COOPERATION AND CONFIDENCE,—these are two very
important resources. Moreover, one is dependent
upon the other. One is the hatchet, while the other
is the handle; one is the lock, while the other is the
key. If the allies will cooperate and have *confidence*
in their leaders, we will be invincible; but otherwise
our cause is lost."

NEED OF CONFIDENCE TODAY

It is probably true that "confidence" becomes a hackneyed subject whenever employment conditions are not satisfactory. It might be said of confidence, as Mark Twain used to say about the weather: "Everybody talks about it, but nobody does anything about it." The employer demands that labor should have confidence in him; while the worker demands that the employer should have confidence in labor. The Catholics demand that the Protestants unite with them; while the Protestants insist that the Catholics should come over into their camps. Farmers appeal to the city people to cooperate; while the city people feel that the farmers should cooperate. Even Mussolini is rattling his sword with one hand, while holding out an olive branch to England with the other. Republicans in the United States are urging the need of confidence, while they are doing their utmost to undermine confidence in the Democrats.

When the Japanese-Chinese conflict was at its height, I was traveling across the ocean in the steamship Berengaria. Two Japanese had steamer chairs near me on the deck. One was a banker from Tokyo and the other was a colonel in the Japanese army. Naturally our conversation would drift often to the situation in China. These two Japanese could see that I was sympathetic with the Chinese. I really think their consciences troubled them. Although they were willing to talk with me, they seemed to avoid the rest of the passengers. When discussing the Japanese-Chinese affair they would always wind up by saying:

"We want to be friends with China, but China will not shake hands with us. We want China to like us, but China doesn't like us. We therefore must force China to like us. This is why we are sending our armies and bombing planes to China."

Since traveling with those Japanese, I have often thought that both two major political parties of the United States are as dense as to how to make friends and establish confidence as were those two Japanese.

FIGURES VS. FEELINGS

My life has been spent collecting and analyzing business statistics. My chief recreation has been the drawing of business charts. One would naturally think that I would believe that the nation's business is ruled by figures. This is not so. I believe the nation's business is ruled by feelings. Kings, Emperors, Presidents, Fuehrers, and Duces think that they are governing. In reality, they are mere marionettes, guided by a string of spiritual and economic forces over which they have little control. This is why history has shown that "the race is not to the swift, nor the battle to the strong." Faith, confidence, credit, and love are the great forces that make for progress and prosperity. Conditions make Presidents; Presidents do not make conditions. The faith and confidence—that is, the *feelings*—of the people determine conditions. This fact cannot be over-emphasized when studying means of eliminating unemployment.

Confidence is a universal force shaping governmental systems in all climes and times. Confidence operates in the United States with especial power. There are two reasons why our governmental system is keenly sensitive to the dictates of the people's faith in the future. The first reason is that ninety per cent of our nation's business is carried on by credit. This is a greater percentage than is true of any other nation. The second reason is that the American temperament is especially volatile. Therefore any realistic and valid discussion of our system of government or general prosperity must be based squarely on a recognition of the great importance of confidence and cooperation. No description of the business cycle and its effects upon both government and employment is complete without serious consideration of underlying spiritual trends. Failure to recognize this fundamental fact is one of the weaknesses which menace the communistic and fascist states. This failure will some day cause the materialistic countries to collapse.

BEWARE OF CRITICISM

This trend toward materialism has worked into our colleges to the great detriment of our national welfare. Many thoughtful people believe that the mechanistic theories being propounded in these colleges are largely responsible for the national unemployment which periodically exists. If this is true, it is not surprising that some Washington Administrations should do some queer things. For many years I have known Franklin D. Roosevelt. I was on a committee representing the Department of Labor when he represented the Navy Department on the same committee. Incidentally, it is interesting to note that Mr. Felix Frankfurter was then the chairman of the committee. That was in the years 1918 and 1919, before Franklin D. Roosevelt had any political ambitions. Yet in those days he always fought for the under-dog. Therefore, I feel it very wrong for his enemies to pretend that his present social theories have been adopted for political purposes. Franklin Roosevelt and his wife have always been interested in making a better and happier world. Their difficulties have come from getting wrong advice as to how this can be brought about.

For this reason, it has been said of him what Oliver Cromwell said over three hundred years ago, that "No one goes so far as he who knows not whither he is going." An English writer said: "Roosevelt's policies revolve with the swiftness of an airplane's propeller. One day he is inflationist; while the next day a deflationist; one day he fixes the prices of gold, cotton, and other commodities, while the next day he bitterly attacks business men for following the same course. One day he urges increased production; while the next day he orders the destruction of food when millions of his people are undernourished. One day he preaches the importance of free speech; while the next day he threatens the political ruin of senators who oppose his measures. He is a severe critic of bureaucracy, and yet he has built the greatest bureaucracy of any American president. He advocates economy, while at the same time is the world's greatest spendthrift. Naturally such a program does not develop confidence." Personally, I believe this criticism to be unjust: Roosevelt at least attempted to find some solution to the unemployment problem.

UNNECESSARY CONFLICTING ELEMENTS

"For the body is not one member but many. If the foot shall say 'Because I am not the hand I am not of the body,' it is not therefore not of the body. If the ear shall say 'Because I am not the eye I am not of the body,' it is not therefore not of the body. If the whole body were an eye, where were the hearing? If the whole body were hearing, where were the smelling? But now hath God set the members each one of them in the body even as it pleased him. If they were all one member, where were the body? But there are many members and one body. The eye cannot say to the hand, 'I have no need of thee'; or again the head to the feet, 'I have no need of you.' Nay, much rather, those members of the body which seem to be more feeble are necessary; and those parts of the body which we think are less honorable, on those we should bestow more abundant honor. . . . God hath tempered the body together—that there should be no schism in the body."

The above was written many centuries ago by a philosopher known as Paul of Tarsus. It is now and always will be true. With the conflicts between industry and agriculture, between employers and labor, between the North and the South, it is very necessary that the nation should recognize that all groups are a part of the same body. When the body is injured, or sick, it usually needs only rest and good food for complete recovery. Poultices, bandages and pills may temporarily revive the feelings of a sick man; but restoration to health comes only from within,—not from without. Confidence, cooperation and consistency must replace contradiction, confusion, and controversy, if the American people are to be fully employed again. When I was giving this explanation once to an old hunter who was tramping the woods with me in Florida, he remarked: "I guess it's a good deal in Washington like down here in this coon country. If you want to make friends with the rabbits, you must chain up the dogs first."

WHAT IS THE ANSWER?

To a statistician the answer is very plain. Partisanship must be abandoned until a normal condition of unemployment returns. If this means that both of the leading national parties must throw over some of their cargo to save the ship, then this cargo should be thrown over. The Party System is sufficient for normal times; the Party System may be the best system for normal times; the Party System, however, is a detriment to the nation during times when there is a lack of unemployment, a dearth of credit, and a general lack of confidence. For the people of the nation to have confidence in one another, they must see that their leaders have confidence in one another. Fear begets fear; but confidence begets confidence, and cooperation begets cooperation.

Confidence and cooperation, however, cannot be secured by merely telling the other fellow that he must cooperate. This means that the wageworkers, as well as the employers, must have confidence,—confidence that they are to have steady jobs at fair pay,—before they will buy as they should. Do not make the mistake of thinking that business men are the only ones needing confidence in order that the wheels of industry may turn as they should. Cooperation and confidence can be secured only as we as individuals take a chance and are willing to run some risk by trusting the other party. Like the Indians of the Charles River, to whom I have already referred, some one must have the faith to build the first canoe.

May we not consider this solution more seriously? Until employment again returns to normal, may we not forget both the words "Republicans" and "Democrats"? Why cannot all groups and sections unite on the words "Coalition Party" or "National Party"? This party would include industry, labor, business, agriculture and every other group, irrespective of former affiliations. Its campaign would be based upon an honest platform, which would make no concessions to regional groups, no pledges to organized minorities, and no false hopes to the unemployed. It would take up the task of rehabilitation unhampered either by unjust political demands or by untried social theorists.

X

WHAT IS A COALITION GOVERNMENT?

A TWOFOLD answer to the question, "What is a coalition government?" will now be given. First, we shall adopt the case method. Let us consider the specific example of how Great Britain met the crisis of 1931 by resorting to a coalition government. Second, let us further sharpen our thoughts on this question by examining in some detail the possibilities of developing a coalition government for the United States as a safeguard and protection in times of emergency. How would such a government be formed, how operated? Those are the points now to be explored. In 1931, the British were staring in the face of a great crisis. In describing this situation and the events that crystallized in coalition, I have checked my own recollections and investigations in England with the scholarly studies edited by Raymond Leslie Buell under the title *Democratic Governments in Europe.**

When the British Parliament adjourned toward the close of summer in 1931, only the shadow of an oncoming crisis lay across the land. Nevertheless, that shadow was sharply defined. Members of Parliament had received and were gradually digesting the Macmillan and May committees' reports. The Macmillan committee had reported that England's financial structure was far from sound. The report of the

* Thomas Nelson & Sons, 1935.

May committee laid bare conditions which portended budget deficiency. The country was shown to be living beyond its means. England also found herself in the tightening grip of radical labor forces which were greatly retarding production and the raising of new capital. The pick-up following the postwar slump had been but a momentary respite. Despite a persistent and disconcerting increase in national expenditure, there were growing symptoms of a gradual hardening of the arteries of employment. Great Britain's amassed wealth was a bulwark against destitution; but economic tides steadily were setting toward another depression.

KING AIDS IN CABINET COUP

Prime Minister MacDonald sought the help of opposition leaders to promote financial soundness. He found them reluctant to come to the aid of the situation, because of their natural feeling that they were not members of the government. He attempted to accomplish something through the economy committee of his own Cabinet. With the assistance of Mr. Snowden, Mr. MacDonald drafted plans for budget balancing by a joint program of severer economies and heavier taxes. In behalf of these proposals he secured the approval of the Cabinet. They were opposed by opposition leaders, together with the bankers. These groups pressed for an alternative, namely: Cutting down the unemployment benefits. This suggestion naturally aroused stiff protest from the trades unions. Thus there was continued pulling and hauling of conflicting interests.

Strained conditions finally approached the point of rupture in late August of 1931. The King now entered to play a rôle. Returning from Scotland, he talked with party leaders and listened to counsel from his financial advisers. Mr. MacDonald held one more Cabinet meeting, which again was abortive. Then he reported at Buckingham Palace that the Cabinet could not agree. On the day following, announcement was made that the King had accepted Cabinet resignations and that Mr. MacDonald was Prime Minister of a "National" government. Shortly thereafter the names of the new ministers were announced. It is interesting to note a statement of Mr. MacDonald's, saying that the new National government was a "government of cooperation" for the sole purpose of coping with the financial crisis. After the emergency had been surmounted, he promised that political parties would resume their normal positions.

COMPOSITION OF NEW "NATIONAL" CABINET

The new cabinet of coalition—or the "National" Cabinet as it was later called—was comprised of ten members. The same positions which they held in the Labor government were retained by the following: Mr. MacDonald, Prime Minister; Lord Sankey, Lord Chancellor; Mr. Snowden, Chancellor of the Exchequer, and Mr. Thomas, Secretary of State for the Dominions. In addition, the new Cabinet contained two Liberals: the Marquess of Reading as Foreign Secretary and Sir Herbert Samuel as Home Secretary. Finally, the total membership of ten was completed by the inclusion of four Conservatives: Mr. Stanley

Baldwin, Lord President of the Council; Mr. Neville Chamberlain, Minister of Health; Sir Samuel Hoare, Secretary of State for India, and Sir Philip Cunliffe-Lister, President of the Board of Trade. Other ministerial offices outside the Cabinet were filled in the main by Liberals and Conservatives.

A study of the first reaction to the new government is very interesting and instructive. It should be recalled that the Prime Minister's own party was the largest in the House of Commons. Nevertheless, most of his old colleagues refused to join the ministry. The Labor party, both in and outside Parliament, lost no time in voicing its dissent. This antagonism speedily spread to other great groups. With every proposal of the coalition government to proceed with the purposes for which it was created, clamor arose from the classes whose toes were trodden on by the announced economies or other measures. There was threat of disorder, riot, mutiny. Thus conditions drifted and bumped along, uneasily and unhappily. The Cabinet decided that the government should go to the country and ask for what was called a "doctor's mandate." By that was meant that the Cabinet was to be the doctor, with authorization to do whatever was judged to be right. Although there were separate Labor, Conservative and Liberal candidates in the field, a great majority endorsed the new "National," or coalition, government with intense ardor. Never before in British parliamentary history had the House of Commons contained five hundred and fifty-eight government supporters and an opposition of only fifty-six. Even Mr. MacDonald confessed that the desired mandate was well-nigh overwhelming in its completeness.

WHAT COALITION DID FOR GREAT BRITAIN

From this case history of coalition actually at work, several useful lessons can be drawn. For one thing, Great Britain's experience shows dramatically the importance of educating the public in advance. Great Britain failed to do this. As a result, endeavors for coalition were nearly thwarted at the outset by social upheavals due to a misunderstanding of coalition, its purposes and its procedures. Fortunately, before it was too late, the British public was educated to the goals at which the coalition government aimed. The example of Great Britain is not adduced as proof that coalition is the sure cure for any crisis. However, the question is often asked, "What is a coalition government?" I have described the British experience as a concrete and realistic answer to that question.

It is worthy of special emphasis that after Great Britain's coalition government had played its rôle with a creditable measure of success, there was a drift back toward the regular party form of government. That is not to be deplored. Perhaps it is to be welcomed. Close followers of the game of football cherish the tradition that the average football squad cannot be brought up to peak form and held there continuously. If violent attempts are made to keep a team at topmost pitch for a whole season, the team tends to crack and slump. The practical policy for the average team is to try for a reasonably good level, and then "point" for the key games. For such games the team can be brought up to peak. It may be that somewhat the same psychology applies to coalition in the present stage of the development of human nature.

To establish and operate a coalition government calls for human nature to rise above its natural level and, at the compulsion of crisis, to attain to unusual heights of character. It may even be that the frailty of human nature would "crack" if attempts were made to keep it constantly at the concert pitch of coalition. One assurance at least may be confidently accepted. In this conclusion we have the support of Great Britain's experience. There is little danger, as pessimists have foreboded, that any coalition government can clamp itself upon a nation as a permanent incubus or old-man-of-the-sea. A coalition in perpetuity? Readers need have no fear of that.

LAYING GROUNDWORK OF PUBLIC EDUCATION

A coalition government is in essence a government rooted in the spirit of cooperation. It is a government in which coalition derives its just powers from the full consent of the coalesced. Therefore, the first part of any program to set up such an emergency government in the United States should be a preliminary drive to educate the public. A dictatorship can be clamped upon a people by force of arms. A one-party rule can be imposed by strength at the polls. A coalition government, however, if it is truly coalitional in substance as well as label, needs the whole-hearted support of all groups and classes. To reach its full effectiveness it must be a grass-roots movement. Many farsighted and patriotic citizens are now sincerely interested in coalition. They view it as a necessary safeguard and protection in times of crisis. These proponents should realize that an indispensable first step is to prepare all groups and classes to *accept* a coalition government. The masses must be taught in advance the significance of such a measure. The conditions which give birth to a coalition government, how it is organized, how operated, and how terminated when its work has been accomplished, must be explained.

MOBILIZING PARTY AND POLITICAL FORCES

Expressed as a theory, a coalition government may be an alliance of Left and Right, Radical and Reactionary, Liberal and Conservative. Developed in practice, a workable coalition may be a merger of kindred elements in existing political parties. Hence to the question, "What is a coalition government for the United States?" we may give answer as follows: It might well be a union of the "Constitutional" members of our Democratic and Republican parties. In fact, various alignments might be practicable and feasible. True coalition requires no ironclad formula. It is not a product of formulas but of realities—plus a reborn instinct for united action and a rekindled willingness to sink partisan selfishness in common sacrifice.

COALITION'S CONVENTION AND PLATFORM PLANKS

Looking toward the more distant future, we may foresee the day when sharp changes will be made in our presidential campaign machinery. When such an era arrives, it will mean this: It will mean that under the menace of an emergency, we shall junk temporarily the parades and tents of the nominating circus. The veneered lumber of partisan party platforms will at times be scrapped temporarily. That is the long view, with its idealism. For the more immediate future it may be necessary and advisable to form a coalition government by using the means nearest to hand. Suppose, for example, that coalition should take the form of harmony between Democrats and Republicans. Then perhaps the most sensible and realistic step might be to let nature take its course. Let such a fusion group hold a traditional nominating convention. Let it build the customary presidential campaign platform. Such a platform could be relatively harmless because the public is now wise in platforms and holds few delusions. The public knows that a platform is plywood: The outer layer is polished to appeal to everybody; beneath are other plies to appeal to as many pressure groups as possible.

PRESIDENTIAL CAMPAIGN FOR COALITION

A similar position may well be taken toward the management of a presidential campaign. In some distant day, this country may have the wisdom to adopt the plan which the writers of the Constitution apparently had in view. When we do that, presidents and vice-presidents will be elected in a genuine and impartial selection by the electoral college, the members of which are chosen by popular ballot. For the present, however, those of us who are working for a coalition government must be content to use ready-made machinery. Therefore, a presidential campaign with such a purpose in view would look much the same as the familiar spectacles of the past. Thus, the formation of a coalition government in the United States would involve campaign songs, political slogans, mass meetings, radio broadcasts, newspaper advertisements,—all the pomp and pageantry. In spirit and character, however, there would be the sharp change and the new appeal.

CABINET MAKE-UP AND OTHER APPOINTMENTS

Under a coalition government there would be the customary Presidential Cabinet. Two changes, however, are implied. First, in making his appointments to Cabinet positions, the President would be under implicit obligations to provide a balance between the two groups of which he has been made the titular head. Under the one-party system, the Presidential Cabinet is frankly, unblushingly *packed*. It is unjust to say that Cabinet posts have always been treated as political plums. A coalition government, however, is one that by its very nature is pledged against plums, spoils and patronage. This is not to propose the fantasy that office-holders will be transmuted into angels by any coalitional magic. It is only stressing the fact that a coalition government, even though it may not become completely nonpartisan, is at least dedicated to become *bipartisan*. Of course, this applies not alone to Cabinet posts but to other Presidential appointments as well. In the second place, under a coalition government, it might be advantageous if somewhat more power were concentrated in the Cabinet. That might facilitate efficiency; and efficiency is one of the keynotes of coalition.

NEW LAWS AND THE JUDICIARY

Those interested in these possibilities have asked themselves the question whether a coalition government would involve much new legislation. This depends wholly upon which method is adopted for forming coalition. If the initial steps were kept simple and practical, not a single new law would be needed to give us a government which in all its purposes, ideals, and effects, would be coalitional. Of course legislative changes might be required if coalition is sought by radical and sweeping methods. This likewise answers another inquiry, whether coalition would affect the judiciary branch of the government. I answer "No," except that special care would be taken to have new appointments satisfactory to all parties. Coalition of the type now visualized implies complete upholding of both courts and Constitution.

CONGRESS AMID COALITION

No delusions need be entertained by anybody who has sat on the sidelines at the proceedings of our national legislative branch. Members of Congress are not inherently less cooperative than members of the

Cabinet, but they are more numerous. In an emergency—and that is the situation for which coalition is designed—the efficiency of any deliberative or administrative body tends to vary inversely with the number of members. A coalition government, if it ever reached its ideal form, would transform not only the Cabinet but Congress. Under those Utopian conditions, both the Senate and the House of Representatives would be combined under a unicameral plan giving justice to both right and left groups. Furthermore, if raised to a visionary level, a coalition government would not be limited to the Federal government alone. Coalition, with its balanced right and left forkings, could be extended throughout state and even local governments. Remember, however, that a coalition government at most is a temporary movement,—an emergency maneuver, adopted for the duration of the emergency only.

HOW WRENCH THE BIT FROM THE TEETH OF A STUBBORN CONGRESS?

Possible objections will occur to the critic of coalition proposals who has seen the frequent spectacle of President and Congress deadlocked into inaction at a time that calls for action. Plainly, it is almost too much to hope that the spirit of a coalition would permeate Congress throughout its entire membership. Coalitionists do not propose dismemberment of the Legislative, Executive and Judicial tripod as established by the Constitution. The tripod in mechanics typifies the maximum of stability with the minimum of mechanism. In setting out a three-point support for our government, the framers of our Constitution built soundly. However, be it remembered that in times of war, the Executive takes over wartime powers and responsibilities. That is strictly Constitutional. May it not be equally within the spirit of the Constitution that a coalition President and a coalition Cabinet may be entrusted with temporary increase of authority in a crisis? Peace hath emergencies no less than war.

AFTER COALITION, WHAT?

Some students of the situation may welcome the promise of coalition to solve an emergency problem, but they may balk at the threat of permanence. To such critics and skeptics it can be pointed out that a coalition has not the least chance of saddling itself permanently on the nation. All history indicates that all fusion movements are generated by the urgency of circumstances. With the passing of this generating crisis, coalition speedily dissolves into its original component, competitive elements. Whatever else it may be, a coalition government is not a thing of permanence. Its very nature is that of an unstable compound. The moment the needed disagreeable tasks have been completed, coalition always tends to revert back to rivalry, competition and partisanship. The tragic but true statement of the situation is that, without the spur of crisis, the trend of human nature is to slip not into coalition but into competition.

DEFINITION OF COALITION GOVERNMENT

Thus we have answered in two ways the question: "What is a coalition government?" First, we have answered the question by explaining an example, the case of Great Britain and the kind of coalition government whereby that nation met a crisis. Second, we have answered the question by a rough blueprint of a coalition government in the United States. We described how such a government might be formed, how composed, how operated. A final answer to "What is a coalition government?" can be given tentatively, as follows: A coalition government is a temporary burying of the political hatchet. For a needed "cleaning-up" process, both parties—or all parties—postpone their party tactics, pool their powers, and thereby perform certain much-needed tasks. For those who prefer their milk of thought condensed into a can no better answer to the question "What is a coalition government?" can be found, perhaps, than the crisp definition in *Webster's New International Dictionary*. A good education is still to be acquired from this prime source, and in it we read:

> "COALITION: A temporary alliance of persons, parties, or states, for a joint action or purpose."

Getting down to practical cases, assume a situation such as that existing in 1938. The natural development is for coalition to come about by the Republicans nominating a conservative Democrat, thus making it unnecessary to have three candidates.

XI

A CHALLENGE TO THE CHURCHES

IN DECEMBER, 1937, an interesting event happened at Seattle, Washington. Three prominent churchmen met there at a public function to "bury the hatchet." The three men consisted of the Reverend Stanley A. Hunter, a Presbyterian minister of Berkeley, California, the Reverend Father Thomas L. Riggs, famed Chaplain of the Yale Catholic Club, and Rabbi Solomon Goldman, of Chicago. They literally dug a hole in the ground and, uniting as one man, buried an actual hatchet! This ceremony was carried out by the National Conference of Jews and Christians. This was founded by men such as Newton D. Baker, good Episcopalian, Professor Carleton J. H. Hayes, prominent Catholic of Columbia University, and Roger W. Strauss, a good Jew. The purpose of this group is "to eliminate a system of prejudice which we have in part inherited and which disfigures or distorts our business, social, and political relations."

There are at least 25,000,000 people in the United States alone who *worship devotedly* the same God and *advocate seriously* the Brotherhood of Man. I make this statement as a statistician. It seems reasonable and conservative, considering that the published total membership figures for the churches of the United States—including Protestant, Catholic and

Jewish—are reported as over 62,000,000. It therefore is very evident that this group could wield tremendous power for good if, in emergencies, these
twenty-five million or more people would work as a
unit. It is with this most important and far-reaching thought in mind that I desire to end this book.
Truly the latent power of this group thrills one,
especially if he happens to be both a statistician and a
churchman. This group, cooperating under sane
leadership, could solve quickly the major pressing
problem of our times,—namely, unemployment.

A FAMOUS SONG

I have a friend, Charles Christian, who tells of attending a great meeting of church people which
closed with the singing of that beautiful old hymn
"Blest Be The Tie That Binds." Readers will remember that famous line which has been sung millions of
time, "Our fears, our hopes, our aims are one." After
coming out of the meeting, he asked: "Do we mean
that? Probably 'our fears are one,' for who has not
fears today in view of the lawlessness, dishonesty
and unemployment rampant throughout the country? But when we say 'our aims are one' and then
go out and arbitrarily divide our votes at the next
election between the two major parties, we certainly
are either very ignorant or a bunch of hypocrites."
Instead of such songs, a prayer might better have
been made asking God to open our eyes really to make
"our aims one." Certainly *in emergencies* church
members should forget the folly of party emblems

and unite their ballots to be a power and blessing to the people of America.

Those who have represented the Church at any political convention have been astonished at the little consideration given by political leaders to the Church's millions of active and devoted members. A small minority of three million members of the American Federation of Labor received far greater consideration, even though the vote of the latter is somewhat scattered. There are two reasons for this: (1) Because the political leaders know that the Church vote will be almost equally divided between the two major parties; and (2) Because the Church group seems to recognize no relation between politics and their religious principles. This may be due—in part—to a reaction from the days when the Church and State were one. It is more likely due to a lack of education on the part of church leaders as to the churchman's duties and responsibilities. Considering the tremendous sacrifices and persecutions suffered by the church leaders of two and three centuries ago, it should be comparatively easy to reawaken churchmen of today to the vital needs of America.

WHAT IS RELIGION?

The foundation of religion, so far as it applies to the Protestant, the Catholic and the Jewish churches, is not theological. The Old Testament is almost void of theology, as commonly presented today, while Jesus Himself had nothing to say about many featured tenets of our churches. He apparently assumed that

His followers would continue with the established
Hebrew Church. It seems reasonable to believe that
He did not visualize a New Testament or else He
would have written something for it. Jesus did little
preaching and, to our knowledge, wrote nothing for
His followers to use as the basis of either a New
Church or a New Testament. Our creeds and dog-
mas started with Paul of Tarsus, although it was two
or three centuries before they were firmly established.
The central appeal of the Old Testament and the
Teachings of Jesus were for Justice, Mercy, and Honesty. Furthermore the Church has grown in influence only when it has fought for these things. The
Church has slipped when these great goals have been
forgotten.

Surely organized religion has been slipping
throughout the world since the World War. What
has happened to the great Roman Catholic Church
in France, Spain, Mexico and other countries is
known by all. The great Orthodox Greek Church
has been thrown bodily out of Russia and other
countries with Russian influence. The Catholic
Church of America has shown some growth both in
numbers and influence; but the prestige of the Protestant and the Jewish churches has steadily declined
since the early 1920's. The accession of new members, church attendance, Sunday School interest, contribution for both home expenses and missions have
all shown sad percentage decreases. Added to these
difficulties, there has been a decline in the character,
courage, and aggressiveness of church leadership.
The men attending theological schools and training
for the ministry, have not the capacity and back-

ground of former days. One reason for this is that we have forgotten that all should unite under one God and carry out His commands.

WHAT I HAVE LEARNED

Since my boyhood days I have always been interested in church work. I joined the church while in High School at Gloucester, Massachusetts. For thirty years I was active in Christian Endeavor and Sunday School activities. Gradually I was called into state and national organization work, although retaining an active interest in the local Congregational Church at Wellesley Hills, Massachusetts, which I regularly attended after moving there. In June, 1936, I was given the greatest honor which my church could bestow, in being elected unanimously Moderator of the National Council of Congregational-Christian Churches. In this capacity I have had an opportunity both to study the one denomination, in which I am directly associated, and to contact the Federal Council of Churches. This latter is a federation of the larger Protestant denominations which I hope will some day include *all* Protestant denominations. Readers may therefore be interested in what I have found and learned. It is this:

Protestantism started in a simple and humble manner with the welfare of the people as its chief goal. When it remained poor, with voluntary workers, it had great influence. This influence would bring it power and wealth, which, in turn, developed a complicated paid organization. This highly developed organization era was followed by a forgetfulness of the people's welfare and a consequent decline in influence. A study of Church history shows that the Church has passed through several of these cycles during the past centuries. Nevertheless, I am happy to note that, however dark the future of the Church has looked at times, it has always emerged from one of these cycles stronger than ever before. Thus, over a long period of time the normal growth line of the Church has been upward, notwithstanding the discouraging pockets into which at times it has fallen. The Protestant Church, the only one about which I can speak with authority, is now in one of these pockets. This is due to many causes, both spiritual and economic. The national leaders of the Protestant denominations are bewildered; they have lost influence with the rank and file of their members; and are on the defensive against those who suggest changes or new methods.

SOMETHING THAT CAN BE DONE

Many laymen feel that paid "organization" work is deadening to the life of most churches. They refer to the way paid officials and secretaries have gradually been substituted for voluntary workers in connection with state and national groups. Shearing the sheep has gradually taken the place of feeding the sheep. Through necessity, these paid officials and secretaries have been forced to devote most of their time to money raising. As a result, our national and state headquarters have become largely business offices run in a competitive way, like a shop or department store. These men and women are even resorting to mail order campaigns and personal appeals as if they were selling vacuum cleaners or oil burners. The support and defense of the *organization* appears to be their big task. The welfare of the people of America has been almost forgotten.

The above condition of the Church may explain why John L. Lewis and other active labor leaders have far greater influence, both at the White House in Washington and in the lowly tenements of our cities than has any Cardinal of the Catholic Church, or the most famous of our Protestant preachers. I did not realize this weakness and the cause thereof until I became Moderator of the Congregational-Christian denomination. In point of numbers this is not a large denomination, although we have six thousand churches and one million members. Yet I constantly think what these one million members and their immediate families could accomplish if seriously united in making a better, more prosperous and happier United States of America. Our little denomination *alone* could have the power of certain very influential minorities now operating at Washington. If only a few of the larger Protestant denominations would cooperate, this one million could easily be raised to over ten million of voters. The Church not only holds the key to solving the employment problem of the United States, but it has the power to use this key at any time.

A DEFINITE SUGGESTION

The Church should not go into politics. The history of both the Catholic and the Protestant

Churches shows that political activity is exceedingly dangerous. The separation of Church and State, in the early days of our country's history, was the result of unfortunate experiences in England during the Sixteenth Century. The difficulties of the Roman Catholic Church in different foreign countries at various times have been due to its mixing in politics. When such movements as the temperance movement have been carried on voluntarily by church workers, real progress towards temperance has been made. When, however, these church workers became politically minded, through the Anti-Saloon League, they went too far and tripped. A reaction which was very detrimental to the temperance movement followed. It is probably wise for the Church to make these three resolutions:

(1) We will never, as a Church, back any one political party.

(2) As a Church we will mix up with state affairs only in emergencies when a great group of the people are suffering.

(3) To re-establish confidence in Democracy and bring about national solidarity, we will, in emergencies, throw the full resources of our membership into electing a coalition government.

A tremendous good could be accomplished by a few of the Protestant denominations taking such a stand. If the leading Protestant denominations would now combine in such a movement with the Catholic and the Jewish Churches, confidence would immediately be re-established, employment would soon be back to normal, and Democracy would again come to its own, *even before the votes* are cast! *The churches have a Faith and the ability to work with Almighty God Who cannot be defeated.* This Power of God, working through man, has developed us from cave dwellers to the civilization of today. We have the same God; faith has the same power; and our people have a greater opportunity, due to present-day education, research, and culture, *than ever before.* We need only to awake and march to victory.

FOREIGN RELATIONS

Those who have traveled in Germany, Italy, and Japan know that an honest feeling exists in those countries that both the Church and Democracy have failed. Mussolini may, at times, be justified when jeering at the people of England, France and the United States as "a wallowing mob." Certainly, true friends of both the Church and Democracy must make both work by putting them back to work in a form so that they can work. This form is Coalition. Coalition is not an impossible dream, a "counsel of perfection" or a political Utopia. Several times in history it has been resorted to by different nations with great success. The difficulty in America, owing to our potent Party System, is that there has been no strong leadership for Coalition. The Church in America is the one group that consistently can render such leadership. America faces two alternatives. We must either resort, in emergencies, to a coalition government or else witness a destruction of the American economic and social system. In the latter case, the churches and the democratic government of America would be superseded by Communism or Fascism. Hence the title of this book is "Coalition Or Chaos?"

Under Coalition all good things are possible, because coalition establishes and maintains the foundation of all good things, namely: CONFIDENCE. Coalition is the essence of Democracy. It is the basic spiritual principle which makes Democracy work. Coalition is what puts the "tick" into Democracy. Unless Coalition is resorted to at times, Democracy will become a mere dream, breaking down under the new impacts of modern conditions. Democracy cannot be made to function in international affairs without, at times, resorting to the vital principle of Coalition. Coalition is the spiritual attitude combined with practical action. Coalition gives to Democracy *works* as well as *words*. Only through Coalition can the dictators of fascist countries be brought to their senses. The churches of America and England have a great opportunity. May it be accepted!

A FINAL THOUGHT

Coalition is the vital force that implements democracy; Coalition is "signing on the dotted line" and the "passing of the papers"; Coalition implants practicability in both Church and State. In normal times the Party System is probably necessary. The Party System, however, can become all that is worst when working in competition. Coalition can become all that is best when working in cooperation. A coalition government best personifies spiritual forces at work in government. For generations, cooperation between different groups and different nations has failed because there has been no practical method of setting up Coalition in emergencies. Coalition gives us a "contract" and puts our religion "in writing." Let me close with one more thought. I am sure that my Jewish friends will be glad to have me quote Jesus of Nazareth.

Just before the Crucifixion of Jesus, He called His disciples together for a Last Supper. At the close of the meal, He gave them His final words. These were said a few minutes before His arrest, which was followed soon by His crucifixion. Here they are, the italics being mine:

> "I am no longer in the world but they are in the world and I come to thee. Holy Father, keep them in Thy name which Thou hast given me, *that they may be one,* even as we are. . . . These things I speak in the world, that they may have my joy made full in themselves. I have given them Thy word; and the world hated them because they are not of the world; even as I am not of the world. I pray not that Thou take them from the world, but that Thou keep them from evil. . . . As Thou didst send me into the world, even so sent I them into the world. . . . Neither for these only do I pray but for them also that believe on me through their word; *that they may all be one;* even as Thou, Father, art in me, and I in Thee, *that they also may be one in us;* that the world may be-

lieve that Thou didst send me. The glory which Thou hast given me I have given to them; *that they may be one, even as we are one;* I in them, and Thou in me, *that they may be perfected into one that the world may know that Thou didst send me* and lovedst them even as Thou lovedst me."—JOHN 17:11-23.